I AM SECOND®

I AM SECOND®

Real Stories. Changing Lives.

DOUG BENDER AND DAVE STERRETT

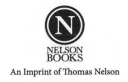

NELSON
BOOKS

An Imprint of Thomas Nelson

© 2012, 2013 by e3 Partners Ministry

Published in Nashville, Tennessee, by Thomas Nelson. Thomas Nelson is a registered trademark of Thomas Nelson, Inc.

Published in association with the literary agency of Wolgemuth & Associates, Inc.

Thomas Nelson, Inc., titles may be purchased in bulk for educational, business, fundraising, or sales promotional use. For information, please e-mail SpecialMarkets@ThomasNelson.com.

ISBN 978-1-4002-0576-9 (TP)

Library of Congress Cataloging-in-Publication Data

Bender, Doug.
 I am second : real stories, changing lives / Doug Bender and Dave Sterrett
   p. cm.
 ISBN 978-1-4002-0373-4
 1. Christian biography. 2. Christian life. I. Sterrett, Dave. II. Title.
 BR1700.3.B46 2012
 277.3'0830922—dc23
 [B]   2011041633

Printed in the United States of America

13 14 15 16 17 RRD 10 9 8 7 6 5 4 3

To the One who is First.

Contents

Foreword

We were both still in college, playing for rival schools. But despite our rivalry, we were friends. More than that, we shared a common commitment. Football was our talent and we loved the game but it didn't define our lives. God was our passion and we wanted our lives to be about him. Not long after Sam interviewed for I am Second, I was able to sit in the chair and share my story.

We gathered in the football team facility of Graham High School. My younger brother, Case, was the quarterback there at the school and my dad was still coaching him, as he always did me. The set was simple: a black backdrop, a single light, a camera and the white chair. I wore a pair of shorts and a black T-shirt. Then I sat down and shared my story. I'm not perfect, nobody is, but like everyone else who have sat in that chair, I talked about how God is first in my life.

Then came the Red River Rivalry, the annual faceoff between the University of Texas and the University of Oklahoma, a game that has been played for over a hundred years between the two schools. Sam was leading the Oklahoma Sooners and I the Texas Longhorns in this classic battle.

The game is always played halfway between the two schools in Dallas, Texas. The stadium itself is split in half, with half the crowd rooting for Texas and the other half for

Oklahoma. Thousands of fans drive up from Austin, and thousands come down from Oklahoma, all to see who will win the big game.

But that year, as everyone drove in, they were met with a question. Lining the highways into Dallas were billboards with our faces asking the question, "Who is Second?" Everyone wanted their team to be first. Everyone wanted their star quarterback to be first. But with the help of I am Second, we were able to tell our fans that no matter who won we were both Second.

"I am Second," is a message we shared then, a message I talk about with my dad in our book, *Growing Up Colt*, and it's one that I continue to share on the national stage with the Cleveland Browns. Second isn't easy. It doesn't guarantee you all the rosy trouble-free clichés you might have heard in school or at church but as I and all those featured in this book will tell you, it is the only way to truly live. Whatever you're facing, whatever your struggle, whatever your hurt or your hope, the stories in this book will give you a glimpse of where to find the answer. And if these stories bring you hope, if they move you, then I encourage you to share them with someone else.

—**Colt McCoy**

Introduction

"Don't do it, Shane," Danny begged. "You've had too much."

But Shane refused to listen. He pulled his motorcycle to a stand. He lifted his leg to mount the bike, but his drunken balance crashed them both to the ground. He brushed off the dust and tried again. Finally succeeding, he roared up the street, leaving Danny in his wake.

Danny downed the last of his drink and left the bar. Feeling an odd compulsion to go for a drive, he borrowed a car and wandered through the neighborhood. In the distance an object lay across the center. As he approached, it proved to be a motorcycle similar to his friend Shane's. Another twenty feet and there lay a man, sprawled across the center line. The street was dark except for a lone lamp glancing off a darkened pool of red that spread under the body.

Danny jumped out of the vehicle and saw it was Shane, lying facedown on the road. His helmet had rolled to the side and his head was broken open. He lay in a pool of dark, dark blood. Danny bent down on all fours and put his face next to Shane's, his cheeks warmed by the touch of his friend's blood.

"Shane, you're going to be okay," he told his friend. But Danny knew it was a lie.

They rushed him to the hospital and into emergency surgery.

"He's still alive," the doctor said, coming out of the operating room. "But he won't be for long."

Danny never disbelieved in God, but he never really believed in him either. His friend was facing death. A man came to pray for Shane, but prayer was never something Danny did either. This was a time of decision. A time to decide if God was someone he believed in, if he was someone he could pray to. Either Danny was a friend and follower of a God who heard his prayers or he wasn't.

As Danny learned, becoming second isn't the journey of perfected saints or of superhero believers. It is the honest, raw, and often painful journey of broken people who have decided that life is not about them. It is not about what they want or about what they can do. Some have tried money; others have tasted pleasure, success, beauty, family, or religion. They all tried something to calm the ache in their soul, to find purpose, love, or happiness. But whatever they tried and whatever they were looking for, they only found it when they surrendered and said, "I am second."

Second is a simple concept. It summarizes all that Jesus taught, all that he lived, and all that he expects from those who claim his name. God is first and others are before ourselves. That is the motto and manifesto that "seconds" live by.

It brings no guarantee of health or wealth, and it makes no promise to take away troubles and trials. Some may describe the rewards of such a life as less tangible. But a smile on your face when the lights go out and a peace in your heart when the storm rages is much more real than any dollar bill or any quick pleasure.

In the following pages, you will see the full gambit of life. Falling in love and facing divorce, healing and sickness, riches and poverty. But in every one of these stories, the lesson is the same. Being second is the only way to find love, peace, joy, contentment, or whatever else you are looking for. It is the only way to find a life worth living. These are the stories of those who have found this to be true.

Rock Stars and Jesus

Brian "Head" Welch

With dozens of tattoos painted across his body, rock star Brian Welch, better known as "Head," sat in the silence of a dark room. Head wore black. He sat in a white chair, with dark eye shadow, long braided hair, white hair ties, and a tattoo of a cross with a tear near his eye. He looked up and told his story.

"Music is everything to me," he said. "Music is my gift.

"I remember after the release of Korn's first album, we were on tour with Ozzy Osborne. During the middle of the tour, our album went gold. Ozzy and his wife, Sharon, gave us champagne after we got offstage. We were surprised, because Ozzy never talked to us the whole tour except for then, but that night, Ozzy and Sharon congratulated us. That's when I first felt like a rock star. It was just surreal. I didn't even know what to say, but it felt good to be a rock star."

Reminiscence flashed across his face. Brian "Head" Welch achieved success. He became one of heavy metal's great lead guitarists. He toured the world with international rock sensation Korn. But he had regrets.

"I worshipped a lot of stuff," Head said. "Worship means love and I loved a lot of things. I loved partying. I loved music. I loved money. I worshipped money. I had been brought up where money was important. Where I came from, you needed money to be respected. If you set yourself up right, then you're all good. I had a mentality where I had to get a certain amount of money so I wouldn't have to worry. Money was my thing."

But money wasn't enough.

"There was a high when I went onstage and saw all these people loving my music and loving me. There were all these girls after me and people worshipping and going nuts for me. I was puffed up on the inside. I started thinking, *I'm important.* That's when the drugs crept in. Cocaine, methamphetamines crept in."

Brian's voice weakened, thinking of the mess his life became. His vision blurred and he looked away.

"At first it was only alcohol, getting drunk," he explained with a quiet pain in his voice. "All of us in Korn drank. We would wait until show time and drink a six-pack. Some of us would start drinking during the show. Some of us would finish thirty beers and we'd be proud of it."

The music blared. The guitar roared. The lights and the volume filled their senses. The crowd screamed for more. The show filled their veins with adrenaline. Head's long braided hair swayed with the thump of the drums and the cry of his guitar. But it wasn't enough. The show would end. And the void would stare at him.

"I couldn't let the night end. I couldn't bear the silence."

That's when the drugs came.

Head looked across the crowd as they worshipped him and his music and thought, *If these people really knew me, they would not be worshipping me. If they got up close, they would see I am just like them.*

"Maybe the drugs were an extension of that feeling of

performance," Head admitted. "Onstage, I was on this high and I did not want to come down. Our music with Korn felt therapeutic, like a cult that the audience would enter just to feel what we felt. I would play and we would scream, and it was a wild, energetic experience. We connected with our fans."

Head thought back to the thousands swaying to his music, cheering at his rifts. His soul wailed through his guitar. The pain of his childhood and the mess of his life vibrated through the strings. His head rocked and his soul ached. But the crowd felt his pain, and knowing that somehow eased the soreness. They were connected.

"Our music was about getting wild and sharing that energy. Our lyrics dealt with abuse, not getting along with the parents, childhood issues, getting picked on. Our fans related. They felt our struggles and they felt synergy and wanted to fight back."

The drugs helped Head hold onto that feeling. They brought relief, but the feeling never lasted. The happiness never stayed. Then he had his daughter. Things were going to change.

"My daughter Jennea came into the world and it was such a euphoric feeling. Jennea was beautiful. I loved her. I thought my life could feel that way forever. The whole thing just felt spiritual. I thought I was going to be happy forever."

Head remembered seeing his daughter for the first time and the feeling of love overwhelming him. But he also loved the attention he got onstage. He loved the yells of the crowd. Soon the long tours and the heavy partying began wearing on his family and on his relationships.

"I was on the road with Metallica, Kid Rock, and System of Down when my wife called. She was freaking out."

"I can't do this," she said with tears in her voice. "When are you going to come home?"

"But I couldn't just fly home in the middle of a tour."

This continued for weeks. She would call, hysterical, begging him to come home. Then the calls stopped. Head tried calling home but nobody answered.

"I started freaking out. I couldn't talk to my daughter," Head said recalling the pain. "I called my home and started threatening the answering machine, until someone finally answered."

"Who is this?" Head shouted. The voice was unfamiliar.

The other end was silent. The stranger wouldn't answer. Panic set in. He had no idea who was at his house. He didn't know where his wife was, and he didn't know where his daughter was.

Days later, a friend who lived down the street called Head. He worked at a nearby pawn shop. "Head, these skinhead punk rock dudes keep coming here trying to pawn Korn equipment that I've seen at your house."

Head was filled with anger and confusion, unable even to go home and figure things out.

One day his wife called again.

"Brian, I'm leaving you," she said. "I don't want to have anything to do with you. I got a guy. He's just a friend, but he's going to protect me from you so you don't hurt me while I leave you."

"What are you talking about? Don't leave!" Head cried.

He felt his life spinning out of control. Memories flashed back of his childhood. His home life was not perfect, but his parents stayed married. Surely, he could make things work with his wife. He thought about his dad. His dad drank a bit.

Sometimes he had anger issues with his dad. They fought on occasion, but they worked it out. Twenty years later, as he held the phone, he was shocked by what his wife was telling him and the coldness of her voice. He convinced himself that he could fix this.

"Don't leave me," he cried. "Look, my parents are still together and I think we can work this out too. I have a three-day break on the tour and I'm coming home. We're going to talk about this. Please, I need you to look me in the eye and talk about this." Tears burst down his face as he pleaded with his wife.

"Brian, I don't want to see you," she responded. "And I don't want to talk with you. I want nothing to do with you. I've got a babysitter that will watch Jennea."

"I became a single father right then," said Head.

From that point on, Head took care of Jennea. She travelled with him on his tours. Head made sure that Jennea was safe.

"Big, beefy security guards would take her on stroller rides while we were on tour," he recalled. "I still drank but not near as much."

Head paused, shook his head, and with shame and anger written across his face, he said, "But I couldn't stay sober. I didn't know how."

Drugs and alcohol soon swept back into his life.

"I had sworn that I would never do methamphetamines again," he said. "I saw what it did to my child's mother. It just took her feelings away and made her leave her own child. I just wanted my wife dead. I wanted to kill her for what she did. I thought my wife was the scum of the earth. How could she do drugs and let the drugs win her like that?"

Even though Head swore he would never do drugs again, he confessed, "I ended up with an everyday crippling addiction to methamphetamine, and everything that I said about my ex-wife came true for me. I sunk to the lowest gutter I could ever think of. I would spend time with my kid and I would still be on it because I needed it to function. I would get up in the morning and have a peanut butter and jelly sandwich and snort meth and then take her to school."

"I told myself that I had everything under control, that I could handle it. But I couldn't. My life was just spinning out of control."

One evening before show time, Head looked at his daughter, Jennea. She was singing. Her little voice was beautiful.

"Wait? What are you singing?" Head could not believe it. His daughter was singing one of his own songs. She was singing "A.D.I.D.A.S., All Day I Dream About Sex."

The full weight of his crumbling life fell on him, "What am I doing? I'm a junkie, my daughter is singing 'all day I dream about sex,' and I'm going to die."

As Head recounted his story, he leaned forward in his chair, stretched out his arms, and screamed. Everyone listening to his story jumped at his burst of emotion. The anger and frustration of so much wasted life overwhelmed him.

But then his face changed. His countenance lifted as he began to talk about his friend Eric, who gave him hope in that dark time of life.

"I don't mean to be weird with you," Eric said with shyness written in his eyes. "I hope you don't take this the wrong way, but I felt the Scripture jump out at me. I've never done this before, so I don't really know how to do this, but I felt like this would mean something to you. It's Matthew 11:28:

'Come to me, all you who are weary and burdened, and I will give you rest.'"

This Bible verse struck a powerful chord in Head's soul. He had tried everything to get pleasure out of this life, but he had come up empty. He reached for the stars and saw his wildest dreams come true. He got more money and more fame than he ever thought would come from playing a guitar. But the burden never left. The hole in his heart never filled. His life spiraled out of control.

He wanted peace. He wanted rest. But he couldn't find it. He thought the path was pleasure, wealth, or success. When his daughter was born, he thought maybe satisfaction was in being a father, but that, too, failed him.

"I remember, all tweaked out, looking up in the dictionary 'weary.' I looked up 'burdened,' and I pulled the Scripture apart."

"I'm weary and burdened, and I need rest for my soul," he said to himself. He felt the verse cry into his soul.

Eric and his wife invited Head to church a couple weeks later. He saw the verse again. The pastor was speaking on it. He felt God calling him. "I didn't know if it was real, but I said a prayer to receive Christ at the church. Then, I went home and did what I always did. I neglected my daughter and took my drugs."

"Jesus, you got to take these drugs from me," he said in one last desperate prayer to God. "Search me right now. Search my heart. You know I want to stop. Take them away. I can't do it on my own."

The phrase "Come to me" rolled through his head. It wouldn't leave. He kept hearing Jesus call out to him.

"Suddenly, I felt like Heaven invaded Earth, all around

me, and I was just in awe of the feeling of ecstatic bliss. I looked up and I was shaking." He felt God. He couldn't explain it. He couldn't define it, but he knew God was there. He knew God heard his prayer.

"Father! Father!" That's all he could get out of his mouth.

"I felt so much fatherly love from heaven and it was like, 'I don't condemn you. I love you. I love you.' It was just love, and instantly that love from God came into me. It was so powerful that the next day I threw away all my drugs, and I quit Korn. I said, 'I'm quitting Korn, and I'm going to raise my kid the right way.' I got the love from God coming into me, and then it came out of me to my kid. It changed me."

Head smiled when he reflected about his daughter.

"My heart was so changed that I said to my daughter, 'Jennea, Daddy's going to be home with you all the time. I'm quitting my career.' And her face lit up; she felt so special."

"God used her to save me," he admitted. When he saw his daughter's life heading down the same path that his life took, he knew he needed to change. He knew he needed help. It was Jennea who helped him hear God's voice. It was then that he finally understood that Jesus offered the purpose and rest he so desperately was seeking.

"When you finally have an understanding that Jesus is everything, and that Jesus can take all that stuff from you and that he takes care of you, you don't have to worry about things anymore. Like, what is life? How did we get here? Where do we go after death? He gives that understanding to you, by faith. He shows you that you're right where you belong, and that feeling is the most incredible feeling in the world and the universe."

"My dream came true way more than I ever dreamed

about. I made more money. I played bigger shows. I had houses, cars. I tried drugs. I tried sex. I tried everything to try to get pleasure out of this life. But in the end it was only God that gave it to me.

"My music used to scream about all my pain in the past. But now I'm screaming about where all the anger and partying got me and how God saved me from myself.

"I thought that I could fulfill my life with all this stuff. I used to think if my dreams could just come true—well, they came true, but they didn't fulfill me. I got so down I just wanted to die. I thought to myself, *What's this life, this life doesn't matter, and who will care if I die? Am I going to get clean and raise my kid so she could be miserable like I am and not have any answers for life?"*

Brian admits that in many ways life after Jesus has been harder. Many of his greatest fans became his critics when he quit the band. But Brian knows Jesus does not offer to take away the noise; what he offers is rest as the city roars and as the night shrieks of trouble. He offers comfort in the middle of the craziness. He offers love, purpose, and meaning. He offers what no one else can. He offers rest.

"But when Christ came in, that feeling he gives is the gift of understanding life. Everything was created by Christ and for Christ. We are created to be with him. Being with Christ is the most incredible feeling because you're where you belong. And contentment is given to you in life because you don't have to look anywhere else and you're exactly where you need to be. And the question about life is answered."

Money will numb the pain, fame will soften the noise, pleasure will hide the terror, for a while. But it won't last. Eventually the screams of pain, the prospect of death, and the terror of every person's failings and longings will waken them to the obvious. Like Head, one day it will all fail and everyone will be left naked in the face of trouble. But Jesus offers rest in the middle of it all.

In 1994 Korn's self-titled album debuted and rose to define the Nu Rock genre of the 1990s. The band went on to win two Grammy Awards and sell more than 30 million records world-wide. After more than a decade with the band, Brian "Head" Welch left the band in 2005 to be a better dad to his daughter.

Watch the Film

Brian Welch
iamsecond.com/brianwelch

To see other stories like this, please visit:

David McKenna
iamsecond.com/davidmckenna

Rod Bayron
iamsecond.com/rodbayron

I Saw
the Sign

Daniel Montenegro

Daniel Montenegro is a twenty-five-year-old Texan. Two large earrings create a hole in each earlobe the size of a quarter. The word *Blessed* is written in cursive across his neck. His appearance was confident and loud, but the tone in his voice was shy. He smiled.

"My childhood was happy. I have a lot of good memories," he said. "I was very close to my family, but things became difficult when my parents separated."

"This isn't an excuse for my bad choices," he paused to clarify. "But sometimes, it got hard without my dad to lead.

"In seventh grade, a friend asked me to smoke pot. I was told in school that drugs were bad and they would kill you. I wanted to try it anyway. I didn't believe anything my authorities in school told me."

Daniel rebelled against authority. He buried himself in as many drugs as possible. He reasoned that if his authorities lied about drugs, what else were they lying about? His progression into drugs continued throughout his high school years.

"After high school, I went to an automotive school and graduated. A coworker eventually introduced me to 'cheese,' a form of heroin. I loved heroin."

Daniel felt guilty for using cheese. He tried to overcome his shame by working hard. But even during his drug use, Daniel was successful at his job and gained respect from his boss and coworkers.

"I was making money, had a girlfriend, but I was disgusted with my life. I knew the cheese had to go. It was hard to quit, but I finally subdued the need for cheese with a lot of cocaine."

The happiness was short-lived and the depression came back. Daniel wanted out of life. One winter night, he was speeding down the road. He was high and drunk.

"I should not have been driving, because I was dangerous."

He saw something that made him slow down. What he saw shocked him, like a ghost in the night. It was a black-and-white billboard with a photo and a simple message.

"I saw the sign and I knew the face on that billboard," Daniel recalled.

The picture was Brian "Head" Welch. In an instant, the picture of the man on the billboard brought back mixed feelings. Years flashed before him. He remembered the first time he used drugs, the loneliness of not having his father. He remembered getting picked on and the anger he felt.

"Since I was about fourteen years old, I've been a Korn follower. They were my favorite band. When depression set in, their music made me feel better. I connected with them."

Korn's music eased the hurt, but only for a while.

"The band grew up and things changed." Daniel recalled the anger toward the man on the billboard. "I hated Head because he left the band. He left because he found God. I thought that was the stupidest reason for him to leave."

"I focused my sight on his billboard picture, threw out my cigarette, turned down the radio, and this time I noticed the words under his photo:

I AM SECOND

"*Must be religious*, I thought to myself. I wasn't sure about it, but I knew that I needed to check it out."

When Daniel arrived home he immediately typed in the web address for "I am Second." He watched a short film of Head's life story. He fought his emotions as he played the film over and over again. The tears flowed.

"I began to weep," Daniel said, "I started sobbing because he summarized my entire life of just being out of control. I knew the pain he felt. He began to talk about Jesus and this love that I had never heard of. As I listened, I knew that I wanted that life."

Daniel decided to go to church. "I felt like the pastor was talking directly to me. He was talking from the book of Psalms," he recalled.

"'The wicked are like grass, they soon fade away,'" the pastor read from Psalm 92:7.

"I knew that verse was like me," Daniel added. "I was the wicked one who was doing wrong. I was like the grass. I was fading away and I needed God."

Two days later he received a call from someone at the church. The man offered to meet with Daniel to talk with him about God. Daniel was not sure if he should meet with the man, but his kind and positive attitude persuaded Daniel to meet him. While he held the phone and listened to the man's eagerness, he remembered the heroin in his refrigerator.

"I remember looking in the fridge where my stash was, then at the door. I was wrestling internally with the decision. Stash? Or the door?"

What was only seconds seemed to drag on for an hour, but Daniel knew he needed to get out of his house.

"I grabbed my keys and drove away from my apartment. I met the man and his friend at the church. He talked with me about Jesus and I prayed to receive Christ. Something in me died at that moment. My life changed. After that, I started living differently. It was a whole new life. Life I never knew existed."

Daniel started going to church on a regular basis and getting involved. His changed life became contagious. He couldn't help but share what he found with others. He felt compelled to talk about Jesus with others. Something inside of him came alive.

"I talked with my roommate about Jesus. He ended up trusting Jesus," Daniel recalled. A smile sprang across his face as he thought of his friend's newfound faith. Excitement vibrated in his voice.

"Dude, you are the last person I ever thought would tell me about Jesus," his friend later told him.

Daniel heard about a mission trip, a trip that would take him to eleven countries in eleven months. The idea of sharing the love of Jesus around the world excited him. So he signed up.

"During our first three months, we went to Africa. I used to be uncomfortable about publicly speaking, but within two weeks of being in Kenya, God gave me great confidence to speak to crowds. One time I spoke to six hundred students. Then we broke up in smaller groups and about twenty students prayed to receive Christ. I felt like God was smiling down on us."

Daniel grinned as he described his journey with God. "God is like the perfect father figure. I started doing drugs very young. I was in middle school. They give you a high for like ten minutes, but compared to eternity, it just isn't worth it. Even as a Christian, I have temptations, but it's not the same as it was before Christ. Another verse I've memorized is 1 Corinthians 10:13. It says, 'No temptation has seized you except what is common to man. And God is faithful; he will not let you be tempted beyond what you can bear. But when you are tempted, he will also provide a way out so that you can stand up under it.' God is good and he will prepare a way for you. If you trust him, he will save you."

Daniel found the forgiveness and purpose that Brian Welch talked about. And he found it all in Jesus. Like Brian Welch, Daniel realized that if he wanted the craziness to stop, if he wanted peace in life and freedom from addiction, he needed God. He could not fix himself. He needed the forgiveness and power of Jesus in his life.

To see other stories like this, please visit:

Lecrae
Iamsecond.com/Lecrae

Resist the
Devil

Josh Hamilton

The field spread around him. Dirt, sweat, and grass stained his uniform. Resin and chalk still colored his hands. Josh Hamilton, "The Natural," "The Hammer," smiled as he strode across the diamond. Blue flame tattoos blazed across his biceps. He released his bat into the dust, donned a black shirt, and sat down.

"I should be dead, with all I have done to my body," Josh said with amazement. The hot Texas wind swirled around the stadium, kicking up the dust from the infield.

"Growing up, I was always great at sports," Josh said with a smile. "Sports were everything. Baseball came before God, friends, everything. When I entered high school, I knew baseball was what I wanted to do with my life. Having a relationship with God, the one who gave me all this talent and love for baseball, was put second."

Josh paused. The silence of the empty Texas Rangers stadium deepened as he looked back over his career. He thought back to a game-deciding moment at the plate. Ten thousand eyes watched as he stepped into the batter's box. The catcher hid his fingers and signaled the pitcher. The pitcher nodded. The ball twirled in the pitcher's fingers. Then came the wind-up and the release. The ball barreled through the air and sank across the strike zone. Josh caught it with the crack of his bat. The crowd jumped to their feet as the ball soared over center field and crashed into the stands. This was what Josh lived for. He lived to hear the crowd roar as he walked across home plate.

Josh was the top Major League draft pick in 1999. He received a record four-million-dollar signing bonus right out of high school. And he was now playing the sport he loved.

"Over those first couple of years, I did well, did really well. And I had more money than I ever wanted to have. My parents were there watching me play the game that they had put so much into. They loved seeing me play."

His parents were always his best fans. But tragedy struck.

"We were on our way home from a spring training game and we were hit," Josh recalled. "A dump truck ran a red light as we were turning left and plowed into us. It was the beginning of what was to come, and what came wasn't anything I ever expected. The two things I really knew in life, baseball and my parents, were taken away from me at the same time."

His parents eventually recovered but had to return to North Carolina for rehabilitation. Josh's injuries took him out of baseball for a month.

"Without baseball and without my parents, I had to find somewhere I could turn where I felt comfortable," Josh said.

"I don't know if you noticed, but I got tattoos." He smiled as he showed his tattooed arms.

"I'd go to the field for two hours in the morning and then I'd have nothing to do for the rest of the day because I couldn't play. So I started getting tattoos and hanging out at the tattoo parlor all day. My parents, for the first time in my life, were gone."

"They always taught me to not hang out at certain places, but I didn't listen." A sense of sadness cracked his voice as he remembered the beginning of a very dark journey. Baseball used to keep Josh busy and out of trouble. He lived and breathed baseball. His mom and dad had always been there for him. Now, Josh was all by himself, and he started trying to fill the void in his life by hanging out with his new friends at the tattoo parlor.

"I was taught that if I was around somebody long enough, I would end up doing what they're doing," Josh said. "But I thought I was better than that. It all started there. I was introduced to my first drug and my first drink. Everyone thought it was so interesting that this clean-cut kid, 'Mr. All-American Boy,' who never did anything wrong, would all of a sudden start drinking and using drugs."

The next four years were filled with drugs, alcohol, and bad decisions. In 2004 he got suspended from baseball for three and a half years.

"The one thing I loved more than anything in my life, I lost it. I didn't have Jesus first in my life. I was trying to do it on my own. I didn't think I needed help from anybody. I was good at everything. But now I had lost my ability to play baseball."

With drugs and alcohol, he found an enemy he couldn't beat. A pitcher whose throws he couldn't hit.

"I just couldn't stop doing it," he admitted. "My second child was born, and even bringing her home from the hospital didn't stop me from going out and using drugs that same day."

"I sank to the lowest point," he said. "I'd barely been married for a year and we separated. My wife couldn't deal with the drugs. I couldn't blame her but it tore me up inside. I had no one left. Drugs and alcohol ruled my life."

During one of those nights in 2005, Josh woke up at two in the morning. He was in a trailer and he didn't know the people surrounding him; they were strangers. He was scared. He didn't know what to do. In that moment he remembered his grandmother, who had always prayed for him.

"I remember showing up at my grandmother's door one night. Grandma had always told me that I could come there for anything. I weigh two hundred thirty pounds now, but I weighed one hundred eighty pounds when I showed up at her door. She barely recognized me because I'd been out for three or four days using drugs. Having to go to her door in the state and condition I was in—" Josh stumbled over his words, and he fought back tears at the memory of being embarrassed and broken as a junkie at the door of his grandmother's house.

"She was always there for me," Josh continued. "I wanted to get better. I didn't want her to see me like that, but I started staying there, and that first week I used drugs a couple of times at her house. She confronted me about it."

Previously, friends and family begged and pleaded for him to stop. "Josh, you're killing yourself. You're killing us by making us worry about you all the time. You're such a good person and you can do such great things," they would say. He couldn't hear it. But something in his grandmother's voice reached his heart.

"Josh, you're killing yourself. Please, stop. Please," she whispered, with tears falling down her face.

"For some reason, God opened my heart that night and actually allowed me to see the hurt and pain in her face and tears coming down her face. That's when I felt like I could do this and I wasn't alone.

"A couple days later I had a dream, and in the dream there was this guy in a dark suit. I was fighting him and I know it was the devil. I was fighting him and beating him and knocking him down. But he kept getting up. I had a bat. I kept swinging it at him. I swung and I swung but could never connect. He had this cold smirk on his face and he just kept getting up and coming after me and coming after me. I was getting to the point where I was worn out and I couldn't fight anymore."

He woke from the dream with a jolt. His sheets were soaked with sweat, his muscles tense, his hands clenched.

"I was twenty-five at the time. I was in the back room. It scared me so bad that I got up out of my bed, went across the hallway into my grandmother's room, knocked on the door, and said, 'Grandma?'"

His head dropped with shame as he knocked on the door. "I had a bad dream. Can I sleep with you?"

"Looking back, it's funny. This was a twenty-five-year-old man asking if he could get in the bed with his grandmother. But it wasn't funny at the time. But she welcomed me in, and the next night I noticed a Bible at the end of the bed.

"I grew up going to church with my aunt and uncle but I never really knew what to do with my faith. I didn't know how to read the Bible, how to pray, how to do all the things it takes to grow closer to Jesus."

When he saw the Bible, he didn't know where to begin. He grabbed the Bible and started fumbling through it. A verse caught his eye.

Humble yourselves before God, resist the devil and he will flee from you.

—James 4:7 NLT

Josh fell on his knees. He was broken. He had nothing left. He had tried to fix everything himself. He tried to do it alone but he failed. He started to pray. He never felt like he knew how to pray, but this wasn't just prayer, this was Josh crying and begging God for help.

"I need help," he cried. "I've been trying to do this for so long and I can't do it anymore. I can't try anymore, because I've failed on my own. So if you would help me do this, I'll do whatever. You do with me what you want to do with me. But I surrender."

He had lost baseball, his marriage was in ruins, and nothing was able to put his life back on track, until now.

"I had to put Christ first before anything would change. And once I surrendered myself to him and told him he could do anything he wanted with me, it all changed. I wasn't the same. He started working on me from the inside. He changed my heart."

Within six months, Josh got back together with his wife and kids and started going to church, reading the Bible, and praying. And he started to train for his return to baseball.

"We moved to Florida so I could get ready to start playing ball again. We were in a hotel room, and I had the dream again. It was the exact same dream. I was fighting the devil, and he was coming after me. I was knocking him down, beating him and hitting him. But he kept getting back up. Then he stopped. He stood there and just looked at me. I looked to my side and though I didn't see Jesus, I knew he was standing right there beside me. I knew it was him because we started chasing the devil and the devil ran away. I woke up feeling more calm and at peace than I ever had before."

Josh started to get back into shape and pleaded to be reinstated into baseball. He was told he would need to submit to drug tests three times a week and prove he could hold a steady job. He got a job working at a baseball academy in Florida. He mowed lawns, unclogged toilets, and took out the trash. When he wasn't working he was working out. He and his wife, Katie, built a system of accountability for him that included Katie, Josh's parents, his agent, several pastors, and others. These individuals talked to Josh regularly and encouraged him.

"They are all Josh's good friends," Katie told the *Dallas Morning News*. "He seeks advice from them, and godly counsel. Pastor Jimmy has been in our lives for many years and is extremely influential. James Robison is someone Josh calls, if not daily, then close to daily."

Eight months later Josh was reinstated. He was picked up by Chicago and then immediately traded to Cincinnati.

After a tour of the minors, a spiral of addictions, and now recovery, Josh finally made his Major League Baseball debut with the Reds in 2007. On April 2 he stepped up to the major league plate for the first time. The crowd roared with a twenty-two-second standing ovation.

As the crowd cheered on, Cubs catcher Michael Barrett said, "You deserve it, Josh. Take it all in, brother. I'm happy for you."

Josh battled with various injuries throughout the season, causing many to believe that his body was irreparably damaged by his four-year drug and alcohol binge. The Reds ended up trading Josh to Texas for the 2008 season. Josh defied his critics by making the American League All-Star team with a career best 130 RBIs, 32 home runs, and a stellar .304 batting average. The Josh Hamilton whom scouts had touted and coaches dreamed about had finally arrived.

But Josh's demons never left. Temptation was always near. On a bitter cold night in January 2009, Katie Hamilton received a phone call from Josh. He was crying on the phone. After three years of being clean, Josh relapsed. He visited a pizzeria that had a bar and ordered one alcoholic beverage. Then he ordered another drink, and then he went to a different bar, where he drank even more. He ended up in some questionable behavior with several women who were at the bar.

"I don't remember everything I did, but they took pictures," he admitted to Katie.

He told his coach, his manager, and the Major League Baseball establishment. Seven months later the photos appeared on the Internet, revealing a drunken, shirtless Hamilton with three young women in the bar. The story caused a commotion on the Internet and beyond. Some disappointed critics blogged that Hamilton should quit baseball. That was when Katie stepped in.

"So many people say they just can't forgive Josh for what he did," Katie said. "But why is it that I, his wife—the one whom he hurt the most by far through this—can forgive him, but they can't? To say something is unforgivable is inaccurate. Anyone can forgive, if they choose to do so. I pray that people can and will, in time, forgive him.

"Josh is a wonderful man, father, and husband who also happens to be human," she insisted. "We are all flawed and that's why we need a Savior. I pray that everyone will understand that he is a very sincere individual with a love for the Lord that is real. Again, he's not perfect. This was a night that he's certainly not proud of, but I am very proud of how he handled it. He was very honest with me and those involved and didn't try to hide anything or cover up his mistake."

Katie continued, "Josh will always have temptation, whether he's in baseball or not. God created Josh to play baseball. To leave baseball because of this one night of defeat would be far more detrimental than staying right where God has placed us. One day he will leave baseball. It certainly doesn't last forever. However, God gave Josh that talent and it's for God's glory.

"This job isn't about money, fame, or being a home run king. None of those things bring happiness, and if that's what it was all about, neither Josh nor myself would be a part of it. What it is about is glorifying God through a talent that he gave Josh and being obedient to the call in which he has placed on our lives, which for right now is baseball. When God takes us out of baseball, he will provide something else for us to do to bring him glory."

Josh continued to work hard on and off the field. He worked for his physical health and his spiritual health. The next season was his best. Josh's All-Star performance against the Yankees helped secure both the American League title for the Rangers and Most Valuable Player of the year. Through injuries, setbacks, and personal struggles, Josh battled back throughout the season. He hit 32 home runs and an incredible .359 batting average, the best of his career.

Josh shares his story of recovery through Jesus with everyone who will listen. "When my addiction was at its worst, Katie told me that one day God would bring me through it and let me play baseball again," Josh recalled.

"But it's not going to be about baseball," she said. "It's going to be about God, and how he brought you to where you are going to be."

"I am reminded of this every time I am in front of the media," Josh said.

"The biggest thing we want to do is to share Jesus Christ with people," Josh told the *Dallas Morning News*. "My whole goal is to do just that with the platform I have been given. Whether I am speaking in public, doing hospital visits to kids during the holidays, or baseball camps, I use baseball as a mission field."

"I believe in Christ," Josh said. "He is first in my life. Family is second. Baseball is second. Everything else comes after Jesus. I wouldn't be where I am today if it wasn't for Jesus. I tried everything. I tried to do it on my own and it almost cost me everything. That is why Christ is first in my life."

Watch the Film

Josh Hamilton
Iamsecond.com/joshhamilton

To see other stories like this, please visit:

David Murphy
Iamsecond.com/davidmurphy

Chris Coghlan
Iamsecond.com/chriscoghlan

James Caldemeyer
Iamsecond.com/jamescaldemeyer

Biggest
Winner

Michelle Aguilar

"I am leaving your father," her mother's voice rang through the phone.

Michelle stopped. Her breath fell short. The words stuck in her ears. She couldn't believe what her mother was saying. Her parents had rarely fought; she had no idea there were problems. So how could her mother just leave? And she didn't even bother to tell her in person. The shock felt like a bad nightmare.

"Why is this happening?" she asked. "Can't you and Dad work this out? Don't you care about my little sister still at home? Don't you care about me?" But nothing her mother said could explain away her questions.

"I didn't know what to do," Michelle said. "I didn't know how to deal with my pain or the confusion that I was going through. I couldn't help but think that her leaving meant that there was something wrong with me, that somehow she was leaving me as well."

"I am going to have to love you from a distance, Mom. I just can't speak to you anymore," she cried to her mother.

At first, she was able to deal with it, to ignore the pain. But soon, loneliness, betrayal, and unforgiveness crept in. Food quickly became a refuge from the growing ache in her heart.

It was an easy step to turn to food. Overeating was the safe sin. People cared if you smoked or got into alcohol, but food didn't seem to matter. And food helped the pain go away.

"If I could just get something really good to eat, then I will feel better," she told herself.

But soon she felt out of control.

"It became a guilt thing. I ate, but eating made me feel worse. I needed comfort, so I ate some more. The food did not bring the comfort I was looking for, so I told myself that I needed to eat more food. It became a vicious cycle."

Her friends and family watched as the weight piled on, but nobody knew of the turmoil that lay beneath. She felt like she was a happy person, but there was a wounded soul behind her smile. She was afraid that if people really knew her pain and her struggles that they would leave her as her mother had left.

Six years passed without Michelle seeing her mother. Michelle gained more than a hundred pounds. Then one day her mom called. She wanted to meet. She wanted back into Michelle's life.

"I wasn't very happy," Michelle confessed. "I was frustrated with all that was going on. But if my mom was going to make an attempt to reconcile, I felt like I needed to make an attempt in her direction as well. After six years I thought I might be ready to start dealing with the pain." She added, "I felt like there were other parts of my life that were spiraling out of control, and if I repaired this relationship, the thing that I felt like started the downward spiral, then maybe that would help fix everything else."

Nothing could prepare her for the journey that lay ahead. The hurt and resentment ran deeper than even she imagined. Michelle thought a few phone calls, an occasional lunch with her mom would let them deal with their issues, but it took a journey to *The Biggest Loser* ranch to face their relational demons head-on.

A friend told Michelle about an opportunity to be on the popular reality TV show called *The Biggest Loser*. This season of the show would highlight families. Two-person teams, composed of severely overweight family members, would compete to lose the highest percentage of weight. Through a brutal combination of team challenges, dieting, national attention, and strenuous workouts led by fitness gurus Jillian Michaels and Bob Harper, contestants would lose weight to win a $250,000 prize.

But money was not what motivated Michelle. She wanted her life to change, to lose weight, and to fix her relationship with her mother.

If I can just go and lose fifty pounds, then that will be enough to come home and feel good about myself, she thought. She wanted to be healthy, but she didn't know what else to do. *The Biggest Loser* seemed to be the answer.

"I felt like I was living half a life, and I hoped that *The Biggest Loser* could bring me to the place where I would be ready to start living a full life."

"I was really nervous," Michelle recalled as she picked up the phone to ask her mom if she would be willing to audition for the show. Her mom agreed to join her for the audition. After countless interviews and rigorous medical testing, the producers fell in love with Michelle, her mom, and their story and invited them to be on the show. They arrived at *The Biggest Loser* ranch and looked around at husbands and wives, brothers and sisters, parents and children, all struggling with their weight and there to make life-altering changes together. They hugged and kissed. Smiled and held hands.

"They all had a really great connection and a really great relationship." Michelle smiled as she scanned the room full of *The Biggest Loser* contestants. But as she turned and saw her mother, the smile drained from her face. "When I looked in the direction of my mother, I saw the source of my pain and I saw the source of my weight gain. Everybody had somebody that they loved and felt really connected with, but I was there with the source of my pain and someone that I hardly knew."

At that moment she realized that this show was going to be more challenging, more personal, than she had imagined.

"I started to do what I always do," she said. "I put a smile on my face, and hoped nobody would notice that I was falling apart inside. My smile was my armor."

If I can just keep smiling, she thought, *and tell everyone that everything is fine, then nobody will know any better.*

She wanted to lose weight and work on her relationship with her mom. But she doubted herself.

"I didn't know if I could do it," she admitted. "And I sure didn't know if I could do it with my mom."

Then Michelle reached her breaking point. On week four of the show, all the contestants filed in to face that week's challenge. They came to a deep pool filled to capacity. Two metal poles hung from special rigging, one for them to stand on and another directly above to hold on to. As each contestant entered the pool and swam to their respective marks, they climbed onto their pole and began balancing the best they could. This was an endurance challenge; to make it more difficult, producers would slowly drain the water from the pool, making it progressively harder to keep balanced. The last person standing on their pole would win the challenge.

The clock began ticking and the water began draining out of the pool. The more water that drained, the harder it became to balance. Michelle's mother was the first to fall into the water. If her team were to have a chance at winning, it depended entirely on Michelle. She held on as long as she could, but her muscles screamed and her patience waned.

"I'm done," she said.

Her broad, beautiful smile masked the pain in her arms and legs. But now Michelle was out. She worked her way down and sat on the bar. After getting the go-ahead from the producers to jump back in the water and exit the pool, she slid off her pole. As she did, the pole swung back. Her head dunked under the water. When she came back up, the pole swung back and hit her square in the mouth, chipping her front tooth.

White, straight teeth and broad, curved lips. Her smile could hide all the pain in her soul. But now that smile was broken. Her tooth was chipped. Michelle immediately burst into tears. It wasn't the pain of a chipped tooth or the aching in her arms and legs; it was her soul being exposed to the world, her armor being stripped away.

"Look at you! Your smile is gone," she felt the world mock at her. "What are you going to do now?"

"I have to get out of here," she cried to herself. "This is too much. I am physically in pain. I'm emotionally in pain. I'm here with the one person who causes me pain. And now I've chipped my tooth. I can't do this anymore."

Uncontrolled emotions swept over her as she swam to the edge of the pool, her mouth hidden behind her hand.

"I can't do this anymore!" she yelled to God. "I can't do

it. I've tried to make it work. I've tried to look happy. I've tried to control everything. But I can't control it anymore. I am totally broken and don't know what to do."

As the challenge concluded, she returned to her room. She sobbed uncontrollably. Her smile was her last bastion of safety, her last defense against the pain that welled up inside her. She had nowhere left to run. God was all she had left. She needed his comfort, his strength. And that is when God intervened. She said one last prayer before she went to bed.

"God, I'm yours. I put my trust in you. I'll do whatever you want me to do. My last defense is gone. I need you. I know I need to forgive my mom, but I don't know how. Show me how. Help me to love her where she is at. I'll love her starting right now. If you want me to stay here on this show, I'll stay here for you. Whether I win this show or go home tomorrow, I will submit to you. God, at the end of the day, when I put my head on this pillow, I want my life to be about you."

As the words fell out of her mouth, her muscles relaxed, her shoulders dropped, and she felt the weight of so much pain fall off her back.

"I was holding on to all the stuff, all the things, all the junk in my life, and then in one collective moment I just let go."

Michelle realized that she no longer had to fight for control. She could trust God. She could love and forgive her mother, without trying to change her. "My relationship with my mom was like my relationship with God. I was going through the motions. I was not completely open and honest with my mom or God.

"Unforgiveness made me sick on the inside, but when I let go, there was a peace that God gave. The God that I loved is the God who forgave me of all my mistakes. I knew if God could forgive me, I could do the same. I knew I could forgive my mom. I think that feeling of peace is just a bonus God gives. A huge burden was lifted off of me."

As the show progressed, Michelle survived to be one of the final four contestants. She continued to remind herself that God was in control. He loved her no matter what. The show, the cameras, dieting and exercising, everything surrounding Michelle focused on her weight and her image. But she was determined that this show and her struggle to lose weight would be about more than how many pounds she lost. It had to be about complete health, spiritual and relational health, in addition to her physical health.

"*The Biggest Loser* is all about weight loss, and many of us can take that as a self-image thing. I was so conscious the whole time of my weight, but I wanted to make sure in those final moments of *The Biggest Loser* that I didn't take it too far.

"I needed to make sure that my self image was healthy from there on out, even after the show. I knew that it really wasn't about the number on the scale that defined me as a person. My identity was in Christ."

Michelle and the other three remaining contestants spent 102 days at the ranch battling their weight, training for a new life, a healthy life. But now they had one last challenge. The challenge was to go home and spend the next four months losing as much weight as possible on their own.

"It seemed so long ago that I packed my stuff to go there and now I was packing up to leave. The person I was on day one was a far cry from the person I was becoming. When I got there, I was not in a good place emotionally. I was living a half life. By the end of the show, I wanted to be the Biggest Loser. But whether I succeeded or failed wasn't the point. I had come so far. I faced my fears. I didn't quit. It was all a sacrifice that was well worth it. I'm a changed person."

Every struggle, every tear, every pain, every sleepless night, every sore muscle was above and beyond what she thought it was going to be. But it was all worth it. She was different. She did exactly what she went there to do.

"You were wildly unhappy," said Jillian Michaels, her trainer, while at *The Biggest Loser* ranch. "You have a lot of challenges that you are going to face when you go home. Hard and challenging things that created this weight problem. But now you know that you are strong enough to face it."

One of the first places Michelle went when she left the ranch was her mother's home.

"Driving up to see my mom was a familiar drive. I used to drive there to drop off my sister. But it never consisted of me coming in and hanging out. So getting the opportunity to come by to see her, to spend time with her, was the first step of this new relationship that we were beginning. This was a huge step for both of us.

"God taught me forgiveness. With my mom I used to associate her with pain and hurt and anger, but now I have been able to forgive her and to love her where she is at."

Her mother was thrilled to have Michelle back in her life.

"I may not be the biggest loser," her mother said with a smile on her face and a tear in her eye, "but I feel like the biggest winner. I am so proud of you, Michelle."

When the time came, Michelle was ready for the finale. She wasn't just ready physically, she was ready spiritually. Her relationship with her mom was healing. Not perfect but better. They had a real relationship.

"I was a changed person. I really, truly began to walk

in love and forgiveness toward my mom. The scale ultimately wasn't going to define me, my weight wouldn't define me, the smile on my face wasn't defining me, but God all along was defining me. To know that I could truly hand it over, hand it over to God, who was in every way big enough to handle everything and that he wasn't going to run away. He wasn't going to see all the junk and run away.

"Me being in control was really me being out of control. So I have Christ first because I know that in him I have a full life. Christ is first in my life because I have tried to live with myself being first. But that life was terrible. It was broken. I have joy and I have peace when I put Christ first. On my own, none of those things are possible."

Michelle began the show weighing 242 pounds and finished weighing in at 132, a total weight loss of 110 pounds. After winning the show, Michelle was able to travel as a Christian speaker for the Women of Faith tour. She appeared on numerous television shows, including *The Today Show* and *The Ellen DeGeneres Show*. Nine days after her victory, Michelle's boyfriend, Micah, proposed and they were married shortly thereafter.

Watch the Film

Michelle Aguilar
Iamsecond.com/michelleaguilar

To see other stories like this, please visit:

Ashley Rawls
Iamsecond.com/ashleyrawls

Victoria Childress
Iamsecond.com/victoriachildress

Bailee Madison
Iamsecond.com/baileemadison

Porn Again Pastor

Nate Larkin

The morning crispness seeped through his jacket. His half-closed eyes craved a warm mug and a bitter coffee. The dark greens and bright oranges of late fall dotted the field in front of him. Trees half emptied of their leaves reached toward the sky as the sun burned through the morning mist. Nate Larkin sat on a wooden bench stained with age and jutted with old paint as he waited for his three friends to arrive.

This was their usual spot, a lonely bench in a secluded corner of Walker's Park. Those worn wooden planks witnessed their weekly confessions and their honest friendship. They witnessed the sharing of wisdom and encouragement, faith and hope. Nate and his friends didn't have a name for the group, not at first anyway. It wasn't a twelve-step meeting or a Christian accountability group, at least not in the conventional sense. But the gritty truth of their broken lives found a voice here every time they gathered. They didn't come to tally their missteps or shame the sinner. They came because they were on a journey together, a spiritual journey. A journey marked with addictions and problems, but a journey they agreed to walk together despite their failings. Or perhaps because of them.

Nate had spent years stumbling through life alone, too ashamed to admit his failures. He fooled himself into thinking he could survive alone. But when faced with the real struggles of life, solitude always failed him. The path wound too steeply and the journey stretched too long. But he didn't always believe this. It took him twenty years of addiction and torment to learn the lessons of honest friendship.

He had always lived two lives, one that everyone saw and one they didn't. Hypocrisy is what he calls it now, but he had better words for it then: reputation, saving face. He told himself that he needed to be strong, that these were his battles to fight. He thought only he struggled, that he alone stood in the breach. He thought he was protecting the reputation of the church. He told himself that victory was in working harder, praying harder, or getting more information. But they were lies. Lies that nearly cost him everything and brought him into a torrent of pain and disaster that ended with him sitting on this bench.

"I wanted to be a pastor and pastors had to be perfect," Nate admitted. "So I set out to build a reputation and to protect that reputation. That meant that there were parts of my life that I couldn't let anybody see. There were some battles I had to fight alone."

He went to seminary, where he trained to be a pastor, but he also learned an unexpected lesson. His class took a seminary-sponsored field trip to New York City. They journeyed to the red light districts to witness firsthand the exploitation of women by the sex industry. They walked into the porn shops and saw the graphic reality of the forbidden fruit.

"I was shocked by what I saw, disgusted by it," he said. His face twinged and his eyes closed, forcing those first gritty pictures out of his mind. "But I was also fascinated by what I saw. It hooked me deep. I didn't just like porn, I became obsessed with it."

Within days, Nate found himself slipping away from seminary and seeking out a source for this new drug. The claws of addiction sank deeper into his flesh. Each day and every week, the grip got tighter. But it never satisfied. It was never enough. He needed a bigger fix, a stronger drug. The obsession became addiction. Control seemed lost. The addiction sapped his marriage and drowned his will. He never meant for it to get to this, but it did.

"I'll stop next week. I'll stop when I graduate seminary. I'll stop when I get a job as a pastor. I'll stop next year." There was always a reason, always a deadline, always a fresh resolution, but the hook set too deep. He couldn't stop. Porn took Nate to places he never intended to go.

"So before I know it, I'm a pastor, married, three kids, and I'm picking up my first hooker on my way to lead a candlelight service on Christmas Eve. I lost any hope that I could stop what I was doing."

Porn at eight o'clock and in the pulpit by nine o'clock. Barely conscious of his own duplicity, he leapt back and forth between two worlds. The pastor persona lived in an artificial smiling world of no trouble, but the real Nate buckled with guilt and reeked of failure.

"When the lights were on and the church was full, the pastor thing felt so real, but on Monday morning I was another man. I was completely alone. I didn't think there was another man in the pulpit who failed to the degree that I did."

Shaken with guilt and terrified at the thought of being caught, Nate eventually left the ministry. But his behavior grew even worse. "I remember so many times screaming at God as I pulled away from some place I shouldn't have been, banging on the steering wheel, saying 'Take this away! I don't want to do this anymore.'"

But God never answered his prayer. Eventually, he concluded God either didn't care or didn't exist. He preferred to think he didn't care. He couldn't understand God's apparent indifference, his unwillingness to provide a private solution to his private problem. After all, he wanted to be good. He wanted to be the model that people followed, the star people revolved around. He thought being good was what the Christian life was all about, and he wanted to be the best.

"It never occurred to me that God let me wallow in my addiction to show me that I was not good. I was not the star that everybody revolves around. I was a broken man in need of a good and perfect God. But I was too proud to see it."

There was something safe about his addiction. Intimacy, real intimacy, carries risks. People can reject, disappoint, and die. But pornography offered a plastic intimacy without the risk. Every day, he said hello to the woman who wouldn't laugh at him, who found him attractive, engaging. But every day he gave a piece of his soul away. Every day, his heart bled and his mind soured, drifting further away from God, his wife, and others.

In the middle of the night, the craving started. His wife lay beside him but he wanted something else. He slid out of bed and crept to the living room. The glow of the screen, the dancing lights. He returned to his secret love. But he was not alone. His wife walked up and stood behind him. Her sobs broke the silence.

"I looked up and she was there. I don't know how long she'd been standing there, but she was crying."

He apologized. They talked. They cried. They worked it through. But it was deeper than one night's talk. She didn't know the years of addiction, the prostitutes and the hotel rooms. But a few days later she found a condom on the floor in the bathroom that he couldn't explain. This time she didn't cry. She sat him down on the edge of their bed.

"I still love you but I don't like you," she said. "I don't trust you. I don't respect you and I don't believe you will ever change."

Nate says, "That's what it took for me to get out of my private world and find help." For so long he kept up the subterfuge. Saint Nate preached his sermons, raised his kids, and lived a good life. But the real Nate roamed the back alleys and rank hotel rooms. He feared rejection and craved his next fix.

"I thought that I was the only guy, or at least the worst kind of guy, that struggled with sex addiction. I thought my story was unique, but as I searched for help I found brave men that had the same story. I reached out for help and discovered that my story was a common one. I was not alone. The details differed, but the story of addiction and failure was the same. I found that I had been held captive by shame all this time."

These men spoke with freedom and honesty. There was no hiding and no facade, just the bare, ugly truth. Nate found an atmosphere of authenticity, a freedom to speak the whole truth without fear of rejection. These were men who had fought a losing battle of addiction. But it was when they surrendered to God and entrusted themselves to others that they found freedom. The addictions never left them, but they tamed the cravings and regained control of their lives.

"These men showed me the power of walking in truth. I got a taste of freedom each time I shared my story, each time I allowed the real Nate Larkin to speak. The liberty was intoxicating. This freedom came at the price of honesty, but that's a small price to pay. Living in the truth, walking in the light, no matter how other people might perceive it, that's freedom."

For the first time, he began to understand forgiveness. For so long he strived for perfection or at least the appearance of it. He alone knew the depravity of his sins and couldn't see how God could forgive him.

"I don't think I really believed the message of Jesus. I thought it was up to me to be good. I didn't believe that God would forgive me. I begged God to forgive me. Every Sunday I cried and I cried, pleading to him for forgiveness, but I never really thought he gave it to me. Looking back, I see how wrong I was. The forgiveness was already mine. I didn't have to earn it. Every time I confessed and repented, I believe I was forgiven. But I couldn't get past forgiveness into healing. I was fixated on forgiveness, unaware that what I needed most was healing, the healing that comes when we confess our sins to one another."

Addiction is a sickness caused by sin. Discovering forgiveness brought Nate his first taste of healing. The cravings never left. His body still cried for his fix and his mind still rebelled with the images of his drug, but now he had a choice. A choice to say no. With the forgiveness of God and the honesty of a few good men, he could turn off the computer screen and avoid the red light district.

"I was sick and I needed healing, but I only knew one model, the instant kind. I had heard of the lightning bolt experience of addicts who find Jesus and are instantly transformed, but that is not my story. I am still an addict. I still want all the same things. God has chosen to heal me with a different process. For me, God has chosen to have confession be my healing. My healing has been a progressive one, and it has come to me through honest participation in Christian community. I have a freedom today, but that freedom has a very short shelf life. I must get a fresh supply of it every day.

"Healing comes when we confess our sins to another, pray for each other. Sometimes quickly, sometimes slowly, but healing always comes. I was fortunate enough to find some other broken Christians with whom it was safe to tell the truth. They didn't have to raise the alarm that there was a sinner among them. They just welcomed me in as a brother."

His mind snapped back with the arrival of his three friends. The morning light and the cold air brought fresh breath to his lungs. He stood from his familiar bench and welcomed his fellow sojourners. They shook hands and began their trek along the graveled path of Walker's Park—the crunch of rock and sand, the whistle of coming winter, and the confessions of four men dedicated to honest living.

Struggles and temptations, failures and successes, life, family, work and God, these are the topics of their walk. There is no wasted time or wasted words. They talk frankly about current challenges, including invisible moral struggles that so often are concealed by life. They confess their failures and share their experiences, strength, and hope. These raw confessions and open hearts have given Nate and countless men like him the strength to walk in the truth.

"I don't think I ever really met Jesus until I stepped out of my church persona and just became another desperate, broken man," Nate says. "When Jesus walked this planet he didn't hang out a lot with church people . . . He was always most comfortable around ordinary, screwed-up people, like me."

"God never loved Saint Nate," he says. "God didn't make Saint Nate. God made me. Jesus loves me. What was missing from my relationship with God all those years was never God; it was me. When he called, I sent Saint Nate. Today, I know that I can answer his invitation personally; the real Nate Larkin can talk with God.

"I used to have this accountability partner. The idea was I lived my life solo and then I reported to somebody else about my progress. It worked for about a week. But then I just started to lie about everything. I didn't want to lose the friendship. It seemed our relationship was based on whether or not I had a good report to bring back."

But these men were different. It wasn't about some sin report or the struggle with confession. That was part of it, but their relationship was deeper than that. They were there at that park because they loved each other and cared too much to let one another walk alone. They each had different struggles and different habits, but they all were broken.

"There is only one person who has ever taken temptation head-on and won. Only one person that ever did it alone, and that was Jesus. The rest of us have to play team ball. Promising yourself or God that you are going to change isn't sane if you are an addict. And accountability isn't enough; you need brotherhood.

"I'm fortunate to still be married to the woman who saw me through this whole mess. She will tell you today that she's been married to two guys named Nate Larkin. And as hard as those first twenty years were, she'd take them again to get the last ten."

Nate Larkin now spends his time teaching people the honesty he found so freeing. He is author of *Samson and the Pirate Monks* and founder of the Samson Society. He speaks widely on the subject of authentic community.

Watch the Film

Nate Larkin
Iamsecond.com/natelarkin

To see other stories like this, please visit:

David Rodenberg
Iamsecond.com/davidrodenberg

Pete Briscoe
Iamsecond.com/petebriscoe

Richard Ellis
Iamsecond.com/richardellis

Life on the Streets

Karen Green

A lonely tear dripped down Karen's dark face as her mind flipped through the horrors of her younger life. She thinks of those days often, but the rawness never leaves. Certain things can never be forgotten.

"Let's just say it wasn't a happy childhood," she said. When she was six, her parents divorced. She was the oldest of five and ended up living with her mom. Her mom worked two jobs and left the kids in the care of neighbors.

"She left us uncovered," Karen said. "A lot of things happened, a lot of things happened—" Her voice trailed off, still grasping for a place to start her story.

"He told me that I had big, pretty legs," she said. The woman next door worked, but her husband stayed at home. The man often watched Karen and her siblings.

"One day he asked me if he could touch me. It felt funny, but I didn't know it was wrong. I didn't understand."

Too young to know the meaning of his touches, she allowed him to continue. Every time he did, he gave her money. Karen took the money, walked up the street to the corner store, and bought candy. Something in her felt dirty, but she didn't know why. The candy washed it away for the moment, but it kept coming back. Then there came a time when he wanted something more.

"I want you to let me lay on top of you," he said.

"I didn't know what was really going on. I was still just a child. So I let him do it. I was just doing what he asked of me."

It was a muddy sort of feeling. She couldn't tell if it was wrong, but she felt soiled every time he touched her, every time they went to the bedroom. She didn't know if it was her or him or the things he did, but it felt wrong. So she told her mother. Her mother called the police. They talked to the woman next door, but there was no evidence.

The next day Karen's mother still had to go to work but warned her not to leave the house. But she did. She was chasing the neighborhood dogs when she caught sight of the man next door.

"I seen him but I didn't think nothing about it, 'cause I was just a kid." She ran up toward the familiar house where the man stood. As she did, he grabbed a brick and threw it at her face. Her nose bloodied and broke. Dazed and wet with tears, she raced home for help.

"If you would have stayed in the house, it wouldn't have happened," her mother scolded, laying the blame on Karen.

"I felt guilty, like it was my fault because I told on the man." She learned then that if anything else happened, she couldn't say anything. She had to hide it.

"We moved around a lot after that, always in low income apartments. All kinds of things began to happen. But I never told my mom. Men would touch me, but I knew my mom would be angry, so I just lived with it. By the time I reached thirteen, I had a baby myself."

Her mother started to date a man. It wasn't long before

he started making advances toward Karen. But instead of dismissing him, her mother dismissed her. Karen's mother told her she had to move in with her aunt.

"I was sixteen and wanted to go out with my boyfriend, but my aunt wouldn't let me. She told me I couldn't go out with younger guys."

"You have to go out with men that can help you and your baby," her aunt told her. "They have to contribute if they are going to go out with you."

She didn't know exactly what that meant, but she did what she was told. Karen started to go out with her aunt's friends, men much older than her. She was sixteen and they were in their fifties and sixties. But they contributed.

"Well, how much money did he give you?" her aunt would ask each time she went out with a man. They always gave something. Her aunt made sure of that.

"When I left her house, I moved in with a guy. We were together for a while, but then we broke up. From that point on, I went out with older men to survive. They gave me money because I didn't have any other way to live. Men were the way I bought my food. Men were the way that I paid my rent. The street and men was all I knew.

"The dating got worse," she admitted. "I started doing drugs and then I had a habit to support. Weed was first. Cocaine came in time." Drugs crowded out her life. She couldn't keep food in the house. She couldn't maintain anything. Drugs controlled it all.

She had a second child, a son. Her mom took her first child, but this one she was going to raise herself. She did what she had to in order to survive. She moved in with another man who paid the rent.

"I allowed certain things to happen," she admitted. The man gave Karen her first black eye. But the beatings and the black eyes wounded something deeper than skin and bone. Her face still carried the emotional scars as she spoke of those dark days.

"Sure, he took care of us, but it came with a big price," she said, looking back. "I had a habit and he helped to support it. He beat me. He put guns to my head. And my son saw all of it." Her son grew up in the chaos of domestic abuse and criminal addictions. He witnessed the violence and the tragedy of his mother's life. The pattern of life that was set so early in her own childhood began to take shape in his as well.

The man eventually left, but by then Karen's addiction was beyond hope. "I didn't know anything else but to go to the streets and to support my habit, not only my habit, but to make sure my son ate." Without a job or a man to pay for the rent, she was forced into the streets. She sold her body for the money she needed.

But it wasn't enough. She and her little boy roamed the streets, unsure of their next meal. No place to stay. No options left. She found a Dairy Queen and walked in with no money. Her clothes were tattered and foul, her boy's face dirtied with the grime of homelessness. Tears streaked her face as she stumbled to the counter.

"Can you feed my boy?" she cried. She knew it had gotten bad but now she knew how low her life had gone. She had always been able to feed her son, but now even that seemed more than she could handle.

The lady behind the counter had compassion as she saw the ruined life standing before her. The lady looked at Karen with her swollen eyes and her desperate face and told her,

"Anytime your baby's hungry, you bring him here and I'll feed him." The lady's voice cracked as she spoke, moved by the utter sadness of the woman pleading in front of her.

"I knew I had to do something to get my son up off the streets. But I didn't know what to do. The drugs got worse and worse. I remember hearing my son one night when he was supposed to be sleeping. I asked him what he was doing, and he told me he was laughing. But he wasn't laughing, he was crying."

Karen's eyes wet at the remembrance of her son's tears. He knew that his mama was up late doing drugs. He knew what the drugs were doing to her, what they were doing to both of them. But all he could do was cry.

"I took my son to my brother and his wife. I asked them to take care of him. I couldn't anymore. I couldn't even feed him. The streets were no place for my boy. So they looked after him and I went back to the streets.

"I remember being out there. I would stay up four or five days at a time doing drugs. I would say to myself, 'Girl what are you doing?' But I didn't know anything else."

She prayed. That's all she knew to do. She went to the streets, sold her body, and prayed. "God!" she would cry. "Help me. Please, help me. I don't want this anymore."

But she still needed more, more money, more drugs. She went out and walked the streets. A man pulled up with his car. She got in. He pulled out and hit the freeway. Sixty, seventy, eighty miles per hour he sped, swerving through the traffic.

"Turn around. Slow down. I got us a room already," she insisted. "We don't have to go anywhere." He said nothing. He only went faster and farther. Her hand gripped the door.

She pushed her feet into the carpet and her back to the seat. Lights blurred by and the city began to pass. He was taking her out of town. He was getting her alone. He said nothing, just a cold stare and an iron grip on the wheel.

They only do this if they are going to do something crazy to you, she thought. Her mind leapt forward, envisioning the worst. Panic set in. She had to do something. She had to get out. He slowed down to bank a turn. With the car still humming at fifty miles per hour, she forced the door open and threw herself out of the car. Her body dropped through the air and crashed onto the highway. The concrete tore her face and gashed her arm. The unmoving earth broke her body as she skidded across the open road.

Somewhere between the waking and sleeping world she came to a facedown halt in the outside lane. Her lungs burned for air. In a flash, she thought of her son and the life she wanted for him. She forced herself to stand. The highway rocked beneath her unsteady feet. Warm blood ran down her face. She turned around and saw a sixteen-wheeler barreling down her lane. She dove to the side and narrowly missed the collision.

A man across the median saw her lying in the road. He ran across traffic and carried her to safety. The paramedics arrived to take her to the hospital. They stitched her up, but the wounds in her soul still bled.

"A couple of days later I went back to the streets with stitches still in my head. It was bad, real bad. I couldn't break the hold of addiction. I went to treatment programs, one after another, nine in total but none broke the addiction. I would go right back out and hit the streets. I couldn't even take care of my son anymore. He was still at my brother's house. Finally, I just wanted to go to jail. I figured that was the only thing I had left. I knew I had a record and they had enough on me to put me away for years. So I went to the nearest police station and just turned myself in."

"Baby, what's your name?" the officer said.

"Karen Green," she said. "There is a warrant for my arrest."

"I can't find the warrant," the officer said, looking through the computer files.

"Nah, it's there, it's there," Karen insisted. "You have to find it. You just have to." She burst into tears. Her knees buckled and she fell to the ground. She sat in the dust beneath the counter praying that the officer would find the warrant. She thought of the twenty dollars that lined her pocket.

"Just go on back out this door," she said to herself. "Go on out and just get another hit. Just go. They can't even find the warrant." But something inside of her kept her sitting on that floor.

"I found it, baby. I found the warrant," the officer finally said. Fresh tears rolled down Karen's face. Tears of joy. The streets and the drugs, the men and the abuse, it was all going to end. She was going to jail, away from it all. She could hardly see the time they were talking about. But she didn't care. She just wanted off the streets. She wanted to be clean.

"They'll be around to get you in a minute," the officer said. "You just sit there; they'll come get you."

They gave her a court date. She stood before the judge and confessed everything. "I just want to get somewhere where I can get myself together," she pleaded. "I need help, and I'll do anything to get it."

"Ms. Green, the sentence that I'm going to give you is

twenty-five to life," the judge said. "There is a program that I am going to get you into, but you only get one chance. If you make it through the program you can get out early, but if you mess up in any way, you're going to do this whole sentence."

"I was so tired of life," she said. "I was so tired of hurting. I was just so tired. I prayed right then. I said, 'God, whatever you do, I don't want to go back out there the same way I came in. If you are the God that they say you are, then change me.' And I remember that's when my life began to change. That's when I surrendered, because I didn't know nothing else to do."

She was scared. She had been in jail before, county jails, but never prison. This was different, somehow more serious, more grave. Her treatment program started. She had been to programs before, but she had never dealt with the real issues, always the symptoms. She would fight the addiction but never the history, never the childhood horrors.

"I think I cried every day for two months. I began to deal with the molestation and the abuse. I began to deal with all my past experiences."

They made her look at herself in the mirror. She had to stand there and just look. She had never done that before. She had never really looked at herself. "We did that over and over and over. I could see the abuse. I could see the wreckage of my life. I didn't like what I saw, but I dealt with it. I faced all my past experiences. Each one I faced gave me more strength."

They had a spiritual program as well. But she didn't go to that. She didn't do church. But the boredom of prison eventually changed her mind. She sat on the front row trying to block out everything, to put her mind on something else. But as the pastor spoke something moved inside of her.

"When we've been through so much in our life, it covers our souls," the man said. "Our soul becomes dark and covered. But what God does is he peels back the covers. Your soul becomes light, you gain strength."

"God," Karen prayed, "this is what you have been doing. You have been peeling back those layers."

She was moved by what the man said. It seemed to all be making sense. God was peeling back those layers, healing her life. She began to study the Bible, listening to God for the first time. She saw other women get released from prison, but they always came back, maybe a month later, maybe two, but they always returned. She didn't want to come back. She wanted real change. There was a life out there that she could live, a life without drugs and prostitution. She didn't know how to live it, but she wanted God to show her how.

Her release date came. They opened her cell, led her through security, and out the front gate. "Pray for me, Chaplain," she said as their paths crossed. With nowhere else for her to go, they took her to the local Salvation Army. People from her past started calling her, inviting her to stay with them. But she knew she couldn't go with them. She couldn't start back down that road. She feared relapse. She feared going back.

"I've been here before," Karen prayed. "I've been at this point, and each time I failed. You said in your Book that you wouldn't let me fail, that you would keep me. I need your help if that's goin' to happen."

She had been through rehabs before, but this one had to be different. She got her first job. She had never worked before, not a real job anyway. Learning to earn a living and to accept responsibility was a big change and a big chore. But with God's help she did it. She started out cleaning homes. It didn't pay much but it was honest. She soon got another job that paid more, enough to leave the Salvation Army and get her own place.

"Me and my son moved into that apartment, and I can tell you we didn't have nothin'. Nothin' but an egg crate and some pillows to sleep on. A frying pan, a nineteen-inch TV, and each other. I remember rolling off that egg crate and just tellin' God, 'You gotta keep me. You know what I wanna go out and do. You gotta keep me.' And he did. He kept me. Everything I prayed for he gave to me. I knew it was his hand in my life.

"All those years, I was looking for the hole, I was looking for something that I didn't get. I didn't get the affection. I didn't get the love. Rejection was one of the things I dealt with, but when God came in he filled those places. It was a process, but he filled those empty spots. I read in the Bible that Jesus loved and accepted me, that I had been accepted, regardless of what I've been through, what I came from.

"It was a long road. It took jail time, Salvation Army, new friends, a new job—it took a lot to get me straightened out, but most of all it took God. He is first in my life because I'm nothing without him. He changed my life. He changed my kids' lives. They saw how he changed me and they knew that God was real. I still look back on my life and I can't believe what I see. God changed everything."

In 1999 Karen Green started Haven of Hope, a Christian nonprofit dedicated to helping women who work the streets she once called home. She partners with the Dallas Police Department, helping to rehabilitate prostitutes and those caught in the sex industry. Dozens of women have found freedom and healing through her programs and her story. The hungry little boy she once took in to Dairy Queen now works as a youth pastor. Her son has a happy family of his own.

Watch the Film

Karen Green
Iamsecond.com/karengreen

To see other stories like this, please visit:

Tim Ross
Iamsecond.com/timross

Lisa Luby Ryan
Iamsecond.com/lisalubyryan

Jarrett Stevens
Iamsecond.com/jarrettstevens

That Kid in
the Corner

Michael W. Smith

The speakers buzz. Power surges through with each beat and every rhythm. Thousands of singing fans sway and shout. The air pulses with his keyboard and his voice with the band behind him. The early winter coolness warms under the flashing lights and the dancing masses. A euphoric gush of emotion fills his lungs at the close of the song. The crowd shouts and screams. He steps off the stage with a wave and a bow. The rumble of the crowd builds as they await the encore.

"We love you, Michael! We love you, Michael!" The voices of three young women rise above the crowd. His ears catch their calls as he heads back onstage. He turns and sees his young fans. His mind flashes back to his small hometown in West Virginia. He thinks of his first song at age five, the feeling of that first touch of the piano. Music sang in his heart. It was his first love, a pure love. He never dreamed of filling arenas or of recording albums, and he never dreamed that girls would one day be screaming his name.

Man, this feels really good, he thinks. A smile cracks his lips as his eyes fix on those three adoring fans. Just then a hand touches his shoulder. He turns to see an old friend. The man grabs Michael's face and stares him in the eye.

"Give it up, Michael! It's not about you," the man says. Michael snaps back to reality and sees the emptiness that tempted his eyes.

"I've never forgotten that moment," Michael admitted. "It really isn't about me. The tours, the millions of records, the fame, it doesn't bring peace. My hope doesn't lie in being some kind of rock star. All that stuff dissipates. It never lasts. If I sell a million records, I want five million; if I sell five, I want ten. The greatest peace is knowing who I really am. I am a son of the high King of the universe.

"When I was six, I heard the *Beatles* song, 'Hey Jude,' on the radio. I hopped up to my piano, figured it out, and began playing it right there. My parents couldn't figure out how I did it. I didn't really know either. I could hear it in my head. My fingers just knew how to find it on the piano."

The flow and rhythm, the dance of notes in his ears—he knew early on that music was what he wanted to do with his life.

"I remember that famous line from Olympic runner Eric Liddell. People asked him why he ran and he said, 'When I run, I feel His pleasure.' When I lay my hands on the keyboard, that is exactly how I feel, I feel God's pleasure. It is what he made me to do."

Michael gave his life to God as a young teenager. He knew music was a part of that surrendering to God. But he never imagined how big a part it would turn out to be.

"A lot of my friends didn't understand where I was coming from. They thought I was some weird Jesus freak. But it never really bothered me."

He played every chance he got. He sang in choir, played at church, performed for friends and family, whoever would listen. He moved to Nashville to pursue it further. He waited tables and planted shrubs, any kind of job to pay the bills, during the day. At night he played the late night bars and red-eye gigs. But as time wore on, the late night scene, the bars, and the new friends all began to change him.

"I started to play with fire. It started with a drink and then a few more. Then I smoked my first joint. I felt so guilty. But a month later I'm in the thick of it. I got sucked into this thing. I didn't even realize it. I justified it, made myself believe that I was okay. But I wasn't. I went from smoking weed to LSD and cocaine. It happened so fast. It's like my compass just disappeared and I entered this whole other world. And when I finally realized how lost I was, it was too late. I couldn't stop.

"But even in the middle of all that, I still believed in God. It was weird. I would go to these parties, totally high, and end up talking about Jesus to my friends. I knew I didn't belong there. I just couldn't get out of the mess that I was in."

He went home to see his parents when he could, between work and shows. But part of Nashville went with him, the grime and underside of music and partying. He tried to hide it, but his glassy eyes revealed the truth. His parents knew their son was doing more than music.

Depression set in, a dark hole that he couldn't get out of. He avoided people. The parties and the crowds felt different. He didn't want to be around them anymore. He just wanted to be alone, but that made the depression even darker.

"I began to pray that God would do something to get my attention. I didn't even know what I was asking. I just needed to be rescued. I didn't care about the cost. I asked God to put me in a car wreck, break my legs, anything to get me out of this addiction and this depression. Then one night I snorted something I thought was cocaine, but it wasn't. I thought I was going to die, and I nearly did."

He lay at the bottom of the pit without a ladder. His life being snuffed out with drugs. His music hollowed and his friends shallow. He sat alone in his apartment. The sky dark with the deep of night. Shadows cast long across the linoleum floor of his kitchen. The dim sadness lay heavy on his back. A mist filled his eyes, then a tear, then a gush of water. He wailed into the darkness. He slid off his chair, his face scraping the floor. He wallowed in his pain and wept and wept and wept.

"God!" he cried. His mouth could utter no more, but his soul wept all his pain and trouble, his addictions and failures. He cried to God, begging for help, begging for forgiveness. He had gotten so lost. He thought back to the day he first heard the call, the day he knew God had a plan for him and his music. Would God still hear his song? Would he accept the prodigal son back home?

"Right then, I felt the presence of God. He didn't say anything. He just wept. The God of the universe came down and wept with me right there on my kitchen floor. I haven't been the same since. It all changed there.

"I made up my mind right then that I would surround myself with great people. The very next day I got a call from my agent."

"There's a gospel group called Higher Ground," the agent said. "And they're looking for a piano player. Are you interested?"

He said nothing at first. His voice failed. He could hardly believe what he heard.

"Yes! Of course," he finally got out. "I'll take the job." He didn't know the group, but it was a dream come true, touring with a solid Christian band. It was the therapy he needed to be nurtured back to health. Somehow the cravings and the addiction melted away. Eight months into the tour he got his first songwriting contract for two hundred dollars a week.

"I thought I'd died and gone to heaven." He ended up writing songs for rising star Amy Grant. His songs made it onto her album *Age to Age*. The album went platinum, the first Christian album ever to do so, and earned her a Grammy for the Best Contemporary Album of the year. People started to notice that Michael W. Smith had a talent for writing music.

His success led to a record deal of his own. His first album contained the hit song "Friends." The album went gold. He began opening for Amy Grant but soon found himself headlining his own tour. His second album earned him a Grammy for Best Gospel Performance.

"I never wanted to be a rock star. I love the platform, I love to sing for people, but my desire was always to just play music for the rest of my life if I could. That's all I ever really wanted. I didn't want all the money or even the fame. I just wanted to play music. I had no idea that I would be playing in stadiums or filling arenas around the world.

"When I was given that platform, I wanted my music to be more than entertainment. I wanted it to inspire people to get out of the four walls of church and challenge them to be the hands and feet of Jesus. We can sing worship songs till we're blue in the face, but if we're not changing the world, we've totally missed it. There is a passage in the Bible that comes to mind."

If you do away with the yoke of oppression,
With the pointing finger and malicious talk,
And if you spend yourselves in behalf of the hungry
And satisfy the needs of the oppressed,
Then your light will rise in the darkness,
And your night will become like the noonday.
The LORD will guide you always;
He will satisfy your needs in a sun-scorched land
And will strengthen your frame.
You will be like a well-watered garden,
Like a spring whose waters never fail.
Isaiah 58:9–11

"God wants more than religious dedication. He wants us to be light in a dark world. Stepping into the gutter and helping the poor and the orphans and the widows—those are the things that really resonate with the heart of God. Those are the things that really inspire my music. That is why I sing.

"I don't wake up every day thinking, *I've got a musical career*, or *I'm going to go make a record today*. There are a lot of things I love about my life, and music is one of them, but I just as much enjoy loving on people. I love finding that kid in the corner, the outcast. I love going up to that kid, putting my arm around him, and loving him. I could do stuff like that for the rest of my life and not sing another song and be very content."

Today, Michael W. Smith is one of Christian music's most recognizable singer/songwriters. His twenty-two albums have sold more than ten million copies, earning him three Grammys and thirty-eight Dove Awards. In 1994 Michael founded Rocketown, a ministry that reaches out to "that kid in the corner."

Watch the Film

Michael W. Smith
Iamsecond.com/michaelwsmith

To see other stories like this, please visit:

Jason Castro
Iamsecond.com/jasoncastro

Blake Mankin
Iamsecond.com/blakemankin

Wally
Iamsecond.com/wally

Brian Welch
iamsecond.com/brianwelch

Michelle Aguilar
iamsecond.com/michelleaguilar

Bethany Hamilton
iamsecond.com/bethanyhamilton

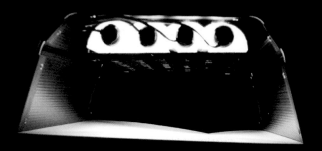

Michael W. Smith
iamsecond.com/michaelwsmith

Whispering Danny
iamsecond.com/whisperingdanny

Brian Sumner
iamsecond.com/briansumner

Ken Hutcherson
iamsecond.com/kenhutcherson

Chris Plekenpol
iamsecond.com/chrisplekenpol

Laura Klock
iamsecond.com/lauraklock

Shannon Culpepper
iamsecond.com/shannonculpepper

Vitor Belfort
iamsecond.com/vitorbelfort

Tamara Jolee
iamsecond.com/tamarajolee

Norm Miller
iamsecond.com

My Other Father

Shannon Culpepper

The dark sky was broken by sparkling lights and the lighted moon. They tossed their napkins on the grated table. Their stomachs were full and their smiles bright. He grabbed the bill and dropped a tip as he stood from his chair. She slid her chair back and stood to follow. It was deep fall and the cool air filled the outdoor café. It buzzed with young love and old friends. They began to walk out into the night. She clung softly to his arm.

"Good night," the hostess called. "Come back again." They nodded to her recited farewell.

"How about a movie?" he asked as they passed onto the sidewalk.

She hadn't told him. She didn't know how; she knew he wouldn't like it. She didn't mind a movie or coffee or a walk or anything else he might suggest. But she never had any space. No place to breathe. He always wanted her with him. Her friends and her family saw less and less of her. Her friends were mad at first, hurt that she seemed no longer to care about them. But that passed. They gave up. Her friends no longer called. Tired of the constant rejection, they stopped inviting her.

But tonight was different. She wanted time with her friends. She wanted time with other people. She loved him, or at least she thought she still did. But she felt suffocated, like she couldn't get away. Even now, she felt the anxious pull in her heart thinking about how she would tell him that tonight she had plans and they didn't involve him.

"I don't know, I think I might just go home," she said, trying to hide the truth.

"Yeah, we can just hang out at your place," he suggested.

"No, I might see some of my friends after I get home."

"We can go together then," he said. "That will be fun."

She paused. Her head dropped, looking for an escape. Brown leaves crunched under her feet. A dampness still clung to sunken corners of the pavement. She knew what was next. He was forcing it. She would have to tell him.

"I think tonight it just needs to be me and my friends," she said. Her breath braced for the emotional blow he was sure to cast.

"Oh, okay." he said. He was quiet. Hurt. Insulted. He let the air fill with guilt and pain. *He's mad.* She knew it. He wasn't saying it, but it was obvious.

"Why don't you want to hang out with me?" he finally said, breaking the silence.

"I do want to hang out with you," she insisted. "But I need to spend time with my friends too."

"You see them all day in class and on campus. This is our time. Why can't you make us a priority?"

"A priority? We just spent all day together," she insisted. "You called when I woke up. You waited for me outside of school. We had lunch and dinner together. We were together all day. I need to see my friends sometimes too."

"You don't think I have friends I want to see? But I make us a priority." His voice quaked with anger. He wasn't yelling, but he might as well be. The bitterness in his voice tore at her heart. His pace quickened. She hurried beside him. The sidewalk ended and dumped them onto the street. He began to cross with her still gripping his arm.

"You are a priority. But tonight I need to be with my friends," she repeated.

"Fine!" he snapped. He grabbed her arm and threw it off of his, jerking his shoulder away from her side. He hurried to his car across the road.

"Go hang out with your friends!" he yelled back at her. She stalled in the middle of the road. Her shoulders dropped and her arms hung limp at her side. Tears ran down her face and the street lights glared off her wet eyes.

What just happened? she thought. *What did I do wrong? I just wanted to see my friends.*

Cars whizzed by her on both sides as she stood stunned in the middle of the road. How had she gotten here? How did this happen? How could she have let it get to this point? She wasn't even allowed to hang out with her friends. This was the man who was supposed to love her and adore her, and he left her abandoned in the street.

Her thoughts flashed back to her father. He was never cruel or hurtful, but he, too, had left her. He didn't move down the street or to the other side of town. Dad moved six hundred miles away to another city in another state.

"I was confused. I would sit and wonder where Dad was. He was so far away I couldn't even picture his new home in my head. I really didn't know how to process it all. I felt like he was in another world. I wondered if it was my fault, if he still loved me, if he still thought of me as his daughter."

She was seven when he packed his things and drove away.

She tried to call, tried to be a good daughter, but it was different now that he was so far away.

"I craved his attention. He was still my dad and I missed him. When I got to see him, he always told me how much I'd grown. I told him he shouldn't have to see me grow up in segments, that he should be with me all the time. I felt like it wasn't fair. He went off, started a new family, got a new wife, had new kids, and I was left out. I felt like I was his second family. They got to spend all the time with him, live with him. But I was first. He had me before he had any of them. I felt so lonely. I cried and cried. So many nights were spent weeping in loneliness."

The years passed and high school approached. She started to date.

"My senior year I fell madly head over heels in love with this older guy. He was smart, beautiful, and successful. It seemed like he had done everything."

He owned his own home, had written a book, and was a fantastic dancer. He seemed perfect. Everything that she had wanted to accomplish in life, it seemed that he had done it, and done it better than anyone else.

"We were so in love. And it wasn't long and we were engaged. But I sacrificed a lot of myself in that relationship. He was very controlling. I had to buy an entirely new wardrobe because my clothes weren't good enough for him. They didn't meet his standards. He got angry if I wanted to call my girlfriends or spend time with my family. I wanted to go to my prom, but there was no way he was going to let me. He accused me of cheating several times. I didn't know how that was even possible; I was with him every moment of every day. I always convinced myself that he was so protective because he loved me. I needed that love. I was trying to fill a void in my life, the love my dad never gave me.

"I poured more of myself, more of my energy into making the relationship work," she said. "But it was never enough. I was never good enough for him. He constantly told me that I wasn't trying hard enough to make things work. It was painful. I remember crying out to God at night, just begging for the pain to go away. I needed to know that I was loved, that he cared.

"It all climaxed that night as I stood in the middle of the road, watching him drive off without me. I knew then that our relationship wasn't healthy. Friends had tried to tell me, but I never saw it until then. We broke up after that, and I became desperate, desperate for love. And God was all I had left."

She searched for answers and searched for love. God is who she found. It happened slowly at first, but soon she realized that God offered the kind of love she had always needed. He was never going to leave. He was never going to move away or abandon her. He would love her forever.

"It was that forever love that I'd been searching for," she said. "It was exactly what I'd always wanted. It was God and not anyone else. It was an overwhelming feeling knowing that God loved me. I certainly didn't feel that I deserved it. But I saw this love in God that went past my failures and my uncertainties. The more desperate and broken I felt, the more love he gave me. He became my other father, the father I never had.

"It taught me forgiveness. I had never really forgiven my dad. He hurt me so deeply when he left, deeper than I ever really admitted. But I wasn't perfect either, and God still loved me, regardless. That was the kind of love that God wanted me to have for my dad. With time, I learned to forgive him for the things he had done. I wanted my dad to know this love that I had found. I wanted him to know God like I did. But he never wanted to talk about it."

Her dad said, "We had to agree to disagree about the whole God thing." He reminisced, "I didn't want it to be the center of our relationship or our conversations. Thirteen years ago I had a motorcycle accident that made me reevaluate my life. I realized then that I was a deacon at church, a Sunday school teacher, even sang in a men's quartet, all because I was trying to please everyone else. I was just doing church because I was supposed to. But it didn't mean anything to me."

Her father spent the next thirteen years of his life running from God. He divorced Shannon's mother, moved to another state, married another woman, got divorced again. He explored the Wiccan religion, agnosticism, and atheism.

"Then Jesus got my attention," he said. "My friend died in a motorcycle accident. I was the first one on the scene.

"I didn't sleep well after that," he admitted. "The last thing I would see at night and the first thing I'd see in the morning was my friend's face."

He attended her funeral, where the pastor spoke about God being the God of second and third chances.

"I thought about how many times I'd been confronted by God in the last thirteen years. Every time I would shake my fist and resist him. But I couldn't resist anymore. I sat there with my head in my hands and elbows on my knees and I prayed."

He prayed, "God, I'm fifty-one years old and I've done

plenty wrong. Maybe you can't use me and maybe you don't want me, but I need you. I've made a mess of my life, and if you can, use me."

"God gave me a daughter who never stopped praying for me," he admitted. "It's because of her and what God has done in my life that our relationship is changing."

Shannon and her dad had struggled in their relationship for thirteen years. He had left so many years ago and the scars still ran deep in Shannon's soul. She felt the pain and the distance. But for the first time, her father began to see the destruction he had created and he wanted to change. His newfound faith gave him the strength to do it.

Shannon and her father still live six hundred miles apart, but their hearts are a whole lot closer. After nearly thirteen years of separation, they are learning to be family all over again. Shannon knows that she has two fathers now, one in Tennessee and one in heaven, and they both love her deeply.

Watch the Film

Shannon Culpepper
Iamsecond.com/shannonculpepper

To see other stories like this, please visit:

Christine Petric
Iamsecond.com/christinepetric

Jack Graham
Iamsecond.com/jackgraham

Priscilla Nicoara
Iamsecond.com/priscillanicoara

The Affair

Jeff and Cheryl Scruggs

"Today you're free!" Cheryl told herself. Her stiletto heels smacked the marble steps as she entered the courthouse. Her attorney met her at the top.

"Today's the day," he said.

She nodded. But she still wondered. Doubt crept into her mind with the solemn echo of the courthouse walls. A battle raged inside her mind with every step. Was this really the right decision? She pushed the thought out of her mind. She had to stay strong. This was not the time for weakness.

The doors to the courtroom swung open. Cheryl and her attorney approached the judge. It took all of her strength to keep from running back through the doors. But she couldn't let this last minute doubt undo all that she had worked for.

"Where is your husband?" the judge wanted to know.

The courtroom felt empty. She stood alone. Her husband never wanted it to come to this. He fought it. With tears he begged for a second chance. But she was tired of feeling empty and unloved. He wanted to fix their marriage, but she wanted out.

"Jeff had to work today," she told the judge. But the judge didn't believe her. He had tried this case a thousand times before with countless couples just like the Scruggs. The proceedings continued to blur by until finally the gavel swung.

"Divorce granted," the judge said with a grimace.

Cheryl had dreamt of this moment. She longed for the relief and joy this moment was supposed to bring, but sadness was all she felt.

Half an hour later she was at Jeff's office with a check for his half of their life together. She tapped the office door. He looked up, his eyes swollen and red. She stepped forward and slid the check onto his desk. He shook his head and said the only thing he knew to say, "I never thought you would actually go through with it."

They had dreamed of happily ever after. They dreamed of growing old together. When they first saw each other in that Memphis eatery, they thought it was forever.

Cheryl tightened her apron, mixed the drink, and hurried to set it in front of her thirsty customer. The smell of alcohol and the sound of chattering patrons filled the air. She glanced toward the door. Her eye caught a man walking in. She stopped. The drink in her hand splashed over the rim. Her heart fluttered and her breath fell short.

Wow! Who is that? Cheryl thought to herself. He looked at her and she looked at him. Their eyes met but neither looked away. She walked up to take his order with her stomach full of butterflies.

"What can I get for you?" she said nervously. The man smiled and ordered his drink. She tried to hide her blushing and keep busy with her orders, but he was all she thought about. The night waned and the building began to empty, but he remained.

"My name is Jeff, by the way. What's yours?" the man asked as she cleared the counter.

"Cheryl." She smiled.

"I don't know if you'd be interested, but I'd love to take you out this weekend."

"I can't," she said, stumbling over her words and looking for an excuse. "I'm busy with school all weekend." She wasn't busy, but she did have a boyfriend. They had been together for two and a half years and marriage was on the horizon. But she didn't want Jeff to know.

Jeff came back week after week, asking the same question. Each time Cheryl stammered for an excuse. But she couldn't stop thinking about him. She couldn't sleep. She couldn't eat. Her mother always told her this is what love would feel like. Seeing the signs and knowing this must be love, she broke up with her boyfriend and said yes to Jeff.

Time seemed to blur by. She graduated from college and went off for training with her company. When she came back, Jeff picked her up at the airport and whisked her off to their favorite restaurant.

They sat down, ordered their food, and started talking. Jeff's knees shook, his hands wet with sweat, but she didn't notice. The waiter came back to their table with a platter. He pulled off the top and displayed a small black box. Cheryl's heart pounded. Her mouth dropped open. She couldn't believe what was happening. Jeff got out of his chair, dropped to one knee.

"Will you marry me?"

"Yes!" she shouted.

Jeff was soon transferred to Los Angeles, where they would start their beautiful Southern California life, together and in love. Barbie and Ken. That's what their friends called them. Jeff and Cheryl had the perfect marriage with all the right trappings. They had dates in Beverly Hills and fine dining in Santa Monica. A fairytale marriage, successful careers, a house on the beach, and all the money they wanted for their California lifestyle.

"My thought of a perfect marriage was one of romance," Cheryl said, "of walks on the beach, cups of coffee, great communication, just my husband and me wedded in bliss. We dreamed of having kids, being successful, having a great home, and all the right things of the world. I thought that was what happiness was. And we had all those things, but something was still missing."

"I would come home and Cheryl didn't seem happy," Jeff said. "I would ask her about it, but she always said she was fine. I thought we were doing great. We had everything we ever wanted."

"I thought maybe it was just time to start our family," Cheryl admitted. "So we got pregnant, very pregnant, in fact. We had two beautiful twin girls. But the emptiness came back. We were doing all the things that a family should be doing, but I was dying on the inside. I couldn't figure out what it was exactly, but something was terribly wrong.

"We got married thinking we could complete each other," she continued, "that we somehow could make each other whole. But I wasn't whole. I felt empty. I was missing something. I got it in my head that it was Jeff's fault, that he wasn't meeting my needs. I got angry because Jeff couldn't understand my pain. The more time that passed, the angrier I got. I never showed it, but on the inside I was emotionally divorcing him, cutting him out of my life."

Cheryl told no one. She locked it all away, refusing to let anyone see her weakness or know her pain. But one day she broke. Tears burst down her face. She wailed in agony. Jeff ran in at the sound of her crying.

"What's wrong?" he asked, rushing to her side, putting his arms around her. But she pulled back, disgusted by his touch.

"I don't know if I love you. I don't know if I've ever loved you." She could hardly believe the words that came out of her own mouth. She never intended to say them, but she felt them. She had for a long time.

"What are you talking about?" Jeff said, confused and hurt. He stepped back and stared in disbelief at her words.

"I'm just so unhappy," she said.

Jeff was blinded to other things as well. Cheryl got a lot of attention at work from the men. She had started to enjoy the attention. She liked hearing how funny they thought she was or how pretty she was. She started thinking about a different life with different men.

One year, she went to her company's annual sales convention. Toward the end of the week, she found herself in conversation with a man who was staying at the hotel. They stood on the veranda talking deep into the night.

"I'm not sure what it is about my marriage, Cheryl," the man said. "I thought my wife and I were going to complete each other, but I feel a distance. We just don't see eye to eye like we used to. I really wish she would understand my feelings."

Cheryl's eyes connected with his as she listened. She understood his feeling. Her marriage was in the same place.

"I just wonder if I married the wrong person," he said. "Do you know what I mean?"

"Yes," she said. She knew exactly how he felt. She wondered the same. If Jeff was the right person, why all the unhappiness, why the distance and the numbness? Why did she feel so dissatisfied? Cheryl and the man continued to talk. The evening turned to night, the night to morning.

"I started to fight what was taking place," she said, looking back. "But I couldn't stop myself. I ended up talking to this man until five in the morning. We didn't do anything physical, but I found myself being emotionally torn away from my husband and being attached to someone else, someone that was paying so much attention to me and delving into my heart."

Cheryl flew home the next day. She felt nervous. Would Jeff be able to tell what had happened? Would he see it in her face? But he noticed nothing. She stepped off the plane and he ran up and wrapped his arms around her. She laid her head on his shoulder. A quiet tear fell down her cheek as she stared off into the distance.

What have I done? she thought.

"I felt like I was two different people living two different lives," she said. "One was a loyal wife, mother, and family person, and the other couldn't stop craving this other man. I could barely function in the home. I cooked, I went to the store, I made love to my husband, but I was gone. My heart was gone from the marriage, and I didn't know what to do about it. And within a month of that first conversation with that man, the relationship became physical."

Jeff soon got a notice at work that he was being transferred to Dallas. They both saw it as a chance to start over, to begin again. Cheryl saw it as a chance to run away and leave the other man behind. But the move only made her feelings stronger. Divorce seemed to be the only option left. What else could she do? She was in love with another man.

One evening, Jeff was reading his daughters a story when

the doorbell rang. It was the sheriff serving him the divorce papers. He took the papers, went upstairs, and finished putting his daughters to bed. Brimming with pain and anger, he hurried back downstairs and found Cheryl.

"What is this all about?" he demanded.

"I don't want to talk about it," she replied.

"What do you mean you don't want to talk? This is our marriage. You can't just walk out. We can get help. We can get counseling."

"But I was cold to him," Cheryl confessed. "I didn't want to talk to him. I didn't want to go to counseling. I didn't want to make our marriage work. So I divorced him on August 21, 1992.

"I was so bitter and so resentful," she said. "I felt like I hated him. I didn't want anything to do with him. I thought divorce would fix everything. But the emptiness never really left. I felt fragmented, and the peace I thought I would have, I didn't have. And the freedom I thought would come never came."

Shortly after the divorce, one of Cheryl's friends invited her to church. She was hungry and searching for something more, something that would fill the emptiness.

"I knew that Jesus died on the cross. I knew that he died for my sins. I grew up saying the 'Hail Marys' and the 'Our Fathers.' But God was always just a religious figure to me. I never felt like I personally knew or connected with God. But the pastor at this church spoke about having a relationship with God. He talked about Jesus filling the emptiness in our souls, and something in that spoke to me.

"I had heard that message a hundred times before. But when the pastor talked about filling the emptiness, I knew that is what I needed. So that day I gave my life to God. And when I did, it all came true. For the first time in my life, that missing link was filled. The emptiness I felt for so long was filled by Jesus. He was what I had been missing all along.

"And in a certain sense that day also became one of the saddest days of my life. I had gotten a divorce because I thought Jeff would fill the hole that only Jesus could fill. I looked behind me and I saw the wreckage I had left behind. I realized that I had made a huge mistake. I wasn't ready for it right away, but I heard God whispering that one day we would remarry. That voice grew stronger and stronger as the years went by. But I never expected it to take as long as it did."

"The divorce brought me running back to Jesus as well," Jeff recalled. "I started going back to church. At church we were studying this book about what it means to be a godly man. And the more I read it the more I realized I wasn't the man I was supposed to be. I was selfish. I was so focused on me and all the things I could get and having all the right toys. I was in my own little world. Even my prayers, what few I had, were selfish. But remarriage to Cheryl was out of the question."

For him, the divorce was final. There was no going back. There was too much pain and too much anger to ever consider remarriage to her. She tore his heart out. This proved even more true when several months after the divorce he discovered Cheryl's affair.

"I was so angry at Cheryl that I couldn't even look at her," he recalled. "I would go over to the house, pick up the girls, and just pray that I wouldn't have to look her in the eye or say anything. I just wanted to get the girls and leave. I blamed Cheryl for everything. I thought it was all her fault."

But something began to change in Cheryl. She said it was Jesus but he didn't believe it, at first. She grew kinder, more gentle. Her smile shone with softness and sincerity, but his anger and pride didn't want to see it. One day Cheryl called him.

"Jeff, I've written you a letter," she said. "I want to come over and read it to you."

"Look, if you want to come over and talk about the girls, that's great," Jeff responded. "But, anything else, I don't want to hear it."

"It's not about the girls. It's about us. I just want ten minutes," she pleaded. He argued but she insisted and begged.

"Okay. Ten minutes," he finally relented. "You can come over and read me the letter. I don't know what kind of response you're wanting from me, but I just want you to know, I still don't trust you."

Cheryl went over and sat down. She shook as she looked at this man whom she had hurt so badly.

How could I make up for what I have done to him? she thought. With tears falling down her face, she read her letter to Jeff. Her voice cracked and her chest heaved with her sobs. Fifteen pages of "I'm sorry." Fifteen pages of regret and sorrow. At the end, she looked up and saw his face wet with tears as well. Maybe this was a sign, she thought. Maybe he felt the same way she did. For an instant she dreamed of jumping up from her chair and running into his arms. She dreamed of walking down the aisle one more time, of starting over, of being a family again.

"Jeff, would you ever consider getting back together?" she asked.

Jeff wiped his tears and laughed.

"No," he insisted. "And don't ever ask me that again. We will never remarry."

"My heart stopped when he told me that," she said. "I was devastated. But in the midst of it all I still felt God speaking to me.

"'I want you to walk with me in this,' God seemed to say. 'My desire is that your family and your marriage be put back together.'

"It was hard for me to imagine how Jeff could forgive me for all the hurt that I had caused. But God showed me a verse in Ephesians that says, 'I can do immeasurably more than anything that you ask or imagine.' I stood on that verse. It became my hope. I prayed that God would allow Jeff to forgive me and that we could start to mend our relationship."

Cheryl never knew, but Jeff kept that letter. He read it every lonely night. He wept as he pondered the words. Remarriage was far from his thoughts, but something in that letter reminded him of the woman he locked eyes with so many years ago in Memphis.

Cheryl began inviting Jeff over for dinner with her and their two girls. But he never came. The betrayal and hurt still cut too deep.

"But God started to change me," Jeff said. "Three years after our divorce, I lay in my bed reading the Bible. I came across a passage in Proverbs chapter three that says, 'Trust in the Lord with all your heart. Lean not on your own understanding. In all your ways acknowledge Him, and He will make your path straight.'

"The divorce humbled me," he continued. "It made me slow down and take a hard look at myself. When I read this verse, I saw all the pride that lay buried in my heart. I saw a hard-hearted man who had always lived for himself and leaned on his own understanding. I began to see why Cheryl must have felt so empty and alone. That night I told God that I would trust him, that he would be first in my life from that moment forward."

After more than a year of Cheryl asking Jeff to dinner, he finally agreed. She prepared a feast, and for the first time in years, the family sat around a table together.

"We continued our family dinners for nearly a year after that night, but I still wasn't ready to get back with Cheryl. I felt like she had to make deposits into my trust account. But the more time we spent together, the more I saw that Cheryl had really changed.

"But our family was still broken. The holidays were particularly difficult. If Lauren and Brittany were with me, they wanted to be with Cheryl. If they were with Cheryl, they missed me. Eventually, our fractured mess became too much for Lauren. There was an outfit she wanted to wear for school one day, and the top was at Cheryl's house and the bottom was at my house. She broke down and started crying and there was no consoling her. One of her friends was over and saw the whole thing."

"Mr. Scruggs!" her friend said with all the sternness her ten-year-old body could muster. Her arms hiked up on her hips and her face scrunched to a scowl. "This is ridiculous. You two get along better than my parents and they're still together. Why don't you just get remarried!"

Wow! Could God use a ten-year-old to speak to me? he thought in the wake of this young prophet's scolding. Pride was indeed what held him back. He knew Cheryl's heart, and if he was honest his heart beat the same. But he never wanted to admit it. The happiest night of his week was with Cheryl and the girls. So one night after the girls were down for bed, he asked Cheryl the question he never thought he would ever ask again.

"I asked you this once before, so many years ago, and I would like to ask you again. Cheryl, I would love to take you out this weekend, just you and me."

Her head dizzied and her heart pounded. Six years of divorce flashed before her eyes. Six years of loneliness and hurt. Memories of lost love and the mistakes of the past. But now she heard what she had wanted so long to hear.

Time flew by as they fell in love all over again. A year passed and eventually Jeff said the words, "I think it's time for us to get remarried." She was overwhelmed. They had been divorced for seven years by that point, and now they were going to be husband and wife again, a family. God put them all back together. On October 3, 1999, Jeff and Cheryl went to Colorado and remarried in the chapel at Beaver Creek.

"I wake every morning with Cheryl beside me in bed, and it's like I have to pinch myself," Jeff said. "I can't believe that our family is back together. Early in our first marriage, our satisfaction came from all the things, all the worldly things, the possessions, the great house with the ocean view. Now we realize that that stuff is just junk. We learned that marriage takes three. Me, Cheryl, and Jesus. We learned that marriage only really works when Jesus is first."

Today, Cheryl and Jeff lead a ministry called Hope Matters Marriage Ministry, helping couples who are struggling in marriages. Their pastor said, "I can't tell you all the life changes that have occurred in our church because of what our great

God and King has done in the lives of Jeff and Cheryl Scruggs. The ripple effect is still roaring through our people. Adultery has been confessed, restoration sought, and healing attained by so many who heard their words. Their story needs to be heard. It is the message of Jesus in action."

Watch the Film

Jeff and Cheryl Scruggs
Iamsecond.com/jeffandcherylscruggs

To see other stories like this, please visit:

The Parks
Iamsecond.com/theparks

Randy Moore
Iamsecond.com/randymoore

Alex Kendrick
Iamsecond.com/alexkendrick

Through Pain or Love

Vitor Belfort

An eight-sided cage awaited their battle. Vitor Belfort, protégé of famed Brazilian Jiu-Jitsu master Carlson Gracie, came to fight in his first Ultimate Fighting Championship (UFC). He faced John Hess, a six and a half foot giant, weighing in at over three hundred pounds. The fight would be Hess's long-awaited answer to his challenge to the Gracie family. Hess's previous fight and UFC debut ended with the technical knockout of his opponent in just over a minute. Vitor was his next target.

The crowd roared in Vitor's ears. His towering foe grimaced from across the octagon. The referee still held the fighters to their corners. In that moment Vitor thought back to the years of training that led to this fight. The sound of iron weights smacking the ground rang through his memories. Punches and kicks from countless sparring partners and competitive foes brought fresh aches to his bones. This was his shot to prove his fighting pedigree. Lose this fight and he risked falling into obscurity; win it and the road opened to a career in fighting.

The bout begins. The referee drops his hand. Hess charges forward, raising his leg to throw the first strike. Vitor rushes in and muffles his opponent's kick. As he charges, Vitor cocks his arms back and then forward, combining his own momentum with that of his opponent's to land a crippling blow to Hess's face. Hess fights to gain back his balance from the blow to his head, while Vitor latches on to his waist. Vitor throws Hess against the ropes, still gripping his opponent's midsection.

They bounce back to center ring. Vitor lurches against Hess's stomach, forcing the back of Hess's leg against his own, crashing Hess to the ground. Vitor climbs on top, firing his muscled arms into Hess's head. Hess flails and kicks in desperate search of an escape from the storm of pain crashing into him. The strikes continue unabated until Hess's arms fall limp and the referee calls the fight. Twelve seconds after the start of the fight, Vitor stands victorious.

"I told God that if I won that fight, I would serve him forever," Vitor admitted. "But I didn't keep my promise. I bargained with God. It was all about me and what I wanted. It took me thirteen years to understand that to be a follower of Jesus, I need to die every day. I needed to kill myself daily. I learned there are two ways to get to God: through pain or through love. It was through pain that I turned back to God."

A year after that initial fight, Vitor suffered a neck injury that threatened to end his career.

"Vitor, you need surgery. But if you get surgery you can never fight again," the doctors said. He went to doctor after doctor and all of them said the same thing. Vitor "the Phenom" Belfort needed to leave the ring.

"I was crying and desperate," Vitor said. "We tried to find a doctor that could fix me without surgery, but they all said the same thing. They all said my career was over."

His mother felt desperate. She couldn't bear to see the

pain of her son losing his dream. She had a pastor come to speak with Vitor.

"Happiness, true happiness, lives inside of you," the pastor said. "Happiness comes from God. Right now you don't have it. You have an injury and you think that unless you can fight you can't be happy. But God will restore you or he will prepare something better for you to do. Trust God for your happiness. Even if you were a poor, homeless man with no legs begging on a street corner, God could still give you happiness."

"I wanted to hear from God," Vitor admitted. "I wanted to have that happiness. That night I asked God to speak to me. I asked him to give me what the pastor was talking about. I hardly slept at all that night. I kept waiting to hear from God, but he never spoke to me."

The next day he was driving to see his physical therapist when he spotted a homeless man on the corner. Stubs took the place of the man's legs. He sat on a tattered platform on wheels, too poor to afford a wheelchair. He wore a plastic bag on his head to guard against the rain. Vitor pulled over and rolled down his window. He stared at the man and thought back to what the pastor had told him. Sadness shown in Vitor's eyes, thinking of his injured neck and his lost career. The man caught Vitor's look and called out to him.

"Why are you so sad?" the man said.

"I was ashamed," Vitor admitted. "Here this homeless man was asking me, a UFC heavyweight champion, driving a beautiful car, with a place to sleep and food to eat, why I was sad. This homeless man beamed with happiness. A smile stretched across his face. Joy seemed to be written in his eyes. But he had nothing. He didn't even have legs to walk on, but he was happy."

"Many people drive by me and think I'm worthless," the man said. "They think this because I don't have a pair of legs. But I can guarantee you that I have more happiness than anyone that drives by here in their big cars, because I got Jesus and Jesus can transform your life."

"I asked God to speak to me and that day he finally did through that homeless man," Vitor admitted.

Vitor continued to look for doctors that could fix him without surgery. He finally found a physical therapist who promised to make him whole again. Six to eight hours a day of therapy and hard work for eight months, and Vitor made it back to fighting. But the injury and the homeless man still weren't enough to bring him back to God.

"I was religious but I didn't understand what it meant to have a relationship with God. I would do religion for six months but then go back to the world. I was going back and forth with God. But you can't play with God like that. That's how you get burned."

Vitor recovered from his neck injury and battled back in the ring. He faced a number of competitors before he got a shot at the light heavyweight UFC title. Randy Couture would be his opponent. He had faced Couture once before and lost. This fight he would have an additional obstacle. A month before the big fight, Vitor's sister went to work and never came home. She was kidnapped. There was no note, no witnesses. Nobody knew what happened.

"We didn't know what happened or where she was," Vitor recalled. "It was like a bleeding that wouldn't stop. Every day we hoped to hear from her or get news that they had found her, but we didn't hear anything. We don't have words for these things. If you lose your husband, you're a widow. If you lose your parents, you're an orphan. But if you lose your child or your sister, there's no name for that.

"I just begged that God would give me the strength to get me through the fight and then I could go home and deal with the whole thing. I started to slowly die. The pain was so intense. I was just losing my faith. I was so mad. I wanted revenge. My heart started to get hard. I had so many questions and nobody had answers. People would try to answer me, but they just had Jesus in a box. Jesus can't live in a box. This was real and nobody had answers."

Vitor faced Couture for the light heavyweight title as promised. The fight lasted just under three minutes and ended with a referee stoppage. A seam from Vitor's glove cut Couture's eye, ending the fight. Vitor Belfort was declared the winner.

Vitor left victorious but broken inside. His sister was still missing. The investigation went on for years, but she was never found. Reports came back that she was raped by more than twenty men and then murdered. Vitor and the Belfort family were devastated.

"I was bitter. I was hurt. I just wanted the pain to stop," he said.

He ended up at the house of a pastor, wanting answers for why life was full of so much pain.

"I am still trying to answer many of those questions myself," the pastor responded after Vitor's torrent of questions.

"What? You don't have answers?"

"No, I don't have all of the answers," the pastor responded. "Nobody does. Only God knows. Right now you don't need answers. You need relief from the pain. And you are not going to get that until you trust God and give him your life."

"Before that day, I was just a religious man," Vitor admitted. "I was just a religious man looking for answers and help. I was so selfish. I didn't want to give anything to God. I just wanted him to fix everything. But that day I realized my selfishness. And I finally started to understand that I needed a relationship with Jesus, not a religion. I needed his mercy and grace and love. I needed the healing that that pastor talked about. I needed Jesus."

"There are two ways to live life. You can choose to live with principle or with preference. If you choose to live for preference, then you live for yourself, you live for the world. But if you live by principle, then God is first. You cannot do both. I'm not perfect. I make mistakes. I get knocked down, but I get back up and keep fighting. I choose to make God first, and I am doing my best to make that a reality in my life. I choose to live second."

Watch the Film

Vitor Belfort
Iamsecond.com/vitorbelfort

To see other stories like this, please visit:

Jason Witten
Iamsecond.com/jasonwitten

Trevor Brazile
Iamsecond.com/trevorbrazile

Driven by Hate

Ken Hutcherson

"I was driven by hatred. Driven!" Ken admitted. "I used to fool people with my smile, but deep down I was one of the most prejudiced people you could ever meet in 1960s Alabama."

It started with his uncle. Ken's father was absent. His grandfather was a drunk. His uncle became his hero, his mentor, his father figure. Ken was five when he got his first lesson.

"Ken," his uncle said, "get outside. I want to tell you how rough your life is going to be growing up and living in Alabama."

He's going to spend some time with me, thought Ken. *He is going to talk to me, teach me something.* Ken didn't know what lay ahead of him, but he was excited. He loved his uncle and couldn't wait to hear what he had to say.

"Okay, I want you to stand right here," his uncle commanded. His tone darkened as he spoke, but Ken suspected nothing. Then his uncle bent down into a football stance.

He's going to teach me something about football, thought Ken. He was elated. He was really going to learn something now.

His uncle grimaced. He leapt toward Ken with all his might. Ken's head plowed into the ground. His feet flung toward the sky. Rocks and dust flew into the air. Pain roared through Ken's little body. The sky spun as he opened his eyes in disbelief.

"Get up!" his uncle roared. "Stand back up! I am not done with you yet."

With tears streaming down his face and his head still throbbing from the tackle, Ken stood back up.

Bam!

Ken flew back to the ground. The same searing pain spread through his body. The same dizzying confusion filled his head.

"Get up!" his uncle yelled.

Again. Again. Again. Six times Ken felt the full weight of his uncle throw him to the ground. His uncle towered over him as he lay stunned on the ground. He bent down, grabbed Ken's collar, and pulled him to his feet.

"Let me tell you something," he breathed in his face. "You are black. You live in Alabama. Whites can never be trusted. You can never be equal. If you're going to do something great, you have to be two or three times greater than any white person in the world. You always have to keep your guard up. You must be better, or they will make you worse."

"My life was changed that day," said Ken. "I believed my uncle, and I graduated with honors in living that life of distrust. I was so mad and so prejudiced."

"In my day, I couldn't go to the front door of a restaurant to order food. We stood outside and ordered through a window out back. We sat in the back of the bus. And we had to like it. At the doctor's office or hospital, white people saw the doctor first. It didn't matter how sick the black kid was. Every time I sat in the back of the bus, I learned to hate a little bit more."

Everything his uncle said began to come true. Football became his outlet. He considered baseball to be his true gift, but football let him hit white people.

"All the times I walked to the back of the bus, all the times going to the back of the restaurant, all the times using the colored water fountain or the colored bathroom, I got it all out in football. I got payback. That first day on the field, I went nuts. I was knocking people down. Stomping them. I was running over folks. They thought I was just this colossal athlete. But they never understood it was the rage pent up inside of me that I let loose on the field. I was filled with frustration. I was a maniac. I hated everybody. Anybody that got in my way, I was going to destroy."

He had dreams of a college scholarship and a shot at the pros, when disaster struck. Ken and a friend were riding a motorcycle when they were sideswiped. The drivers of the car were drunk. The rear bumper of the car slit open Ken's leg from the waist to the knee. He crashed to the ground, bounced off a car, and then stood to his feet. A white woman seeing the whole thing screamed from the sheer intensity of the moment and ran up to see if Ken was all right.

"What in the world is wrong with you?" Ken said to the woman with hate dripping in his words.

"Your leg!" she said, pointing to his bloodied leg.

"It's best if you just leave," he snapped back. "I'm the one that's hurt. Nobody wants you around here."

An ambulance came and transported him to a hospital.

"We're going to have to put you under to sew you up," the doctor said, recognizing the severity of his injuries. There were no black doctors, no black nurses. White people were going to be putting him to sleep.

"No way!" Ken said. "You're not going to put me to sleep. I am going to watch you put every stitch in me." Ken hated white people. He didn't trust them. He didn't want white people sticking needles in him without him knowing about it.

"Son, you got a lot more guts than you got sense," the doctor responded.

He commenced to sew Ken up without anesthesia. Five and a half hours later, Ken was wheeled out of the emergency room. He was told he would never play football again, that his nerves would never fully heal. But he didn't believe them because they were white. He was determined to prove them all wrong. And true to his word, he was back on the field the following year with college scouts in the stands.

But soon white parents grew tired of this black kid beating up on their white kids on the field. They began calling the coaches. "Get that animal off our team!" they screamed. "He is not fit to play with our kids."

But the coaches refused. People decided to take matters into their own hands. Ken and two of his friends were walking home after a game one night. It was dark but three silhouettes stood out in the distance, walking toward them.

"Hey! There could be some trouble," Ken's friend said.

"We can take them!" Ken boasted.

"No, we gotta run," his friends insisted.

"No way!" Ken yelled. "I'm not running from no white person."

"You don't understand, man. Come on. We gotta run!" Desperation ran through his friend's voice. These were the days of lynchings, and being caught surrounded by a group of white people deep in the Alabama night was a bad idea.

"If you're afraid to fight, I can whip all three of these guys," Ken boasted.

"Come here and get your beating, boy!" one of the men in front called out.

"Hey! You guys got a problem with me?" Ken strode toward them and challenged their might. Two of them turned and ran. The other stood his ground.

Suddenly, a bolt of pain struck his body. Someone had snuck up from behind and hit him in the back of the ribs with a rock. The pain spread through Ken's body and he fell to the ground. When he fell, they came in from everywhere, like wolves—kicking, beating, using sticks and rocks.

His mind flashed back to his uncle's lesson, "Whites can never be trusted, Ken!" The words roared through his memories.

Ken screamed for his friends. But it was no use, they were gone.

I gotta get up, he thought. *I gotta fight through this. I gotta break through and run.* And he did. He broke free and started running toward his side of town. He escaped, but not without two broken ribs.

Fighting and violence became a way of life. Teachers and principals thought he was a model student. Honor roll, star athlete, polite, and happy. But behind it all he hid anger and hatred. He beat kids up in the bathrooms and locker rooms. He waited for white kids to be alone in alleys or at night. He burned the homecoming floats and beat up the homecoming queen.

"They never knew I was beating up all of these people. Then I started realizing something. I hated everybody. I didn't even like black people. Anybody that got in my way, black or white, I hated them."

The violence and hatred grew to a boil. The school called an assembly to try to calm the fighting and the bickering between blacks and whites. They couldn't prove it, but they began to suspect Ken was behind a lot of the violence. The whole school gathered in the auditorium. The speaker talked about Boom Boom Bradley, a football player who followed Jesus.

Ken began to think back to something he heard as a boy. He was watching television and a man came on talking about God. Ken didn't know anything about this God person. But something held him to the television.

"One day, everyone will have to face God," the man on the television said.

It shook Ken to know that his life would one day be called into account. That message never left him. It always ate at him. He suppressed it, he tried to ignore it, but it always came back. One day, he would have to explain his life to God. His anger, his rage, and his hatred would all be laid bare. No amount of smiling or excuses would hide his hidden deeds. God would know.

As Ken left the assembly he remembered the speaker's message. The speaker talked about the Bible being God's playbook, and something in that message spoke to him. It made sense. Ken had felt the prejudiced eyes of his world and responded with hatred. Anger fueled his success on the football field and in life. Frustration and rage were his motto. But they left him burning inside. The hatred brought darkness and misery. It was time for a new playbook.

Two of the guys at the school had been praying for Ken for years. Ken lettered in four sports every year, and every day for the last three years these two guys showed up at all of his practices. He didn't know what they were doing there at the time, but later he found out. They would sit in the stands or on the bleachers and they would pray. They knew that if God turned Ken's life around, all that hatred and all that energy would be turned to love. And that would be a lot of love. That day as he left the auditorium, it finally happened. He looked back over the mess that his life had become and he gave his life to God.

"There's got to be something more to life," he reasoned. Anger poisoned his life. He knew no love, no peace, no quiet. He was alone and his anger made him that way.

"God if you're real, here I am. I'm yours."

Ken went home, found a Bible, and began reading it.

"God, I meant what I said. I'm yours. I'm going to give you all of me. I'm going to pick up your Bible, your playbook, and I'm going to study it. I'm going to know how the plays are run, and I'm going to run those plays. My coach doesn't ask my opinion on how to run his plays, and you're not asking me how to run your plays. God, you are now my coach. What you say goes. I don't care what anybody else says. I've made a mess of my life. What others have said has made a mess of my life. You've got to be it."

He began reading his Bible for hours a day. God began to change his life right then. And one of the first things God told him was, "Jesus died for white people too."

"At the time, I didn't know that God had a plan for this stubborn, prejudiced, hateful, unbelieving heathen. Well, I'm here to tell you, I ran into Jesus Christ. And that was the message I heard loud and clear. 'Jesus died for everyone.' Who am I to have a prejudiced thought toward any of God's creatures? Before I became a Christian, it was all about me. It was what I wanted. It was about my revenge. It was about my prejudice. But now, that all changed. I was not first anymore. I was second."

At first nobody believed him. They thought it was impossible that Ken Hutcherson could love white people.

"I used to hate everybody. I even hated Martin Luther King Jr. I thought he was the worst thing that ever happened to black people. Martin Luther King Jr. kept running around saying, 'Non-violence. Non-violence. Non-violence.' Not me! I thought he had abandoned us. But now I realized he was right. We shouldn't hate one another. We needed to love each other."

Students knew the kind of person Ken used to be. But now he was talking about Jesus and about loving everyone, whites included. Nobody liked that message. Hate was the culture of his town. Hate was written on the walls and painted in their hearts.

"I got isolated. I didn't just get isolated for a couple of days or a couple of months, but for years. Nobody wanted to have anything to do with me. The whites still saw me as black, and the blacks saw me as a traitor. They thought I was just trying to get in good with white people by saying I was a Christian."

I got Jesus now, he thought. *Things are going to be smooth.*

But they weren't. They got worse. He had nowhere left to hide. Death threats started coming in, pouring in. The homecoming game was approaching, and he was told if he played they would kill him. They threatened to shoot him right on the field if he played. Police warned him. Coaches warned him. There were so many threats to his life that they said they didn't think he should play.

"My time to go is my time to go," Ken said. "I committed my life to Christ, and if he lets me get killed, that's up to him."

When the game started there seemed to be more police present than fans. Nobody wanted to be around him. Nobody wanted to get shot. Just as the first half came to a close, gunshots ripped through the air. Ken took off running. The crowd scattered. Nobody knew where the shots came from or where they went. But everyone was running. Ken raced toward the dressing room, crashed through the doors, and passed out on the floor. His body hit the ground with a thud. The adrenaline and stress collapsed him to the ground. His teammates rushed in and woke him up.

"This is just too much," they said. "Just stay in the dressing room for the second half."

"No!" he cried. "I've committed this one to God. Let's get out there and play that second half."

They got out to the field, started playing, and guns went off again. The crowd rushed the field. Panic ensued. He was sure the fans were going to get him, but the crowd calmed and dispersed back to the stands. The game finally concluded and Ken ran back to the dressing room, where he collapsed once again out of sheer exhaustion.

"Jesus was sufficient. He brought me through it," Ken said, looking back. Ken stood for love. And God stood with him.

"What became of all that anger?" Ken asked himself. "It got washed away with Jesus. He died to save me. He died because he loved me. And his blood washed away my hate. The love of Jesus changed me, protected me, accepted me, and I will do the same for anyone, no matter what they look like."

As the civil rights movement raged on, Ken continued to speak out against prejudice and hatred. He learned to love and he learned to love white people. In fact, he ended up marrying one.

"Now, that old prejudiced guy married one of the whitest white women around. We've got a cross-cultural family. My wife is of German descent. I'm black. We've got four German-chocolate kids, two boys and two girls—all gorgeous."

Ken was recruited by the University of West Alabama and played starting linebacker for four years. After graduation he was drafted by the Dallas Cowboys and subsequently played with the San Diego Chargers and the Seattle Seahawks, spending five years in the NFL. Today, he pastors a church that is 65 percent white and 35 percent everything else.

Watch the Film

Ken Hutcherson
Iamsecond.com/kenhutcherson

To see other stories like this, please visit:

Tony Evans
Iamsecond.com/tonyevans

Tyrone Flowers
Iamsecond.com/tyroneflowers

Lee Yih
Iamsecond.com/leeyih

Crazy
Beautiful
Thing

Whispering Danny

They boarded with few possessions but packed a wealth of hope. Jews fleeing a hostile land, searching for a home with the medical help their son so badly needed. He had Papillomatosis. Benign tumors grew along the air passages of his throat. Every four months he required surgery to remove the unwelcome growths. The result was a damaged larynx and a halting raspiness in his voice. He became known as Whispering Danny.

Previous generations flooded through Ellis Island by boat. Now they came through the air, but New York still stamped their tickets. Lady Liberty still greeted the hungry masses and the foreign tongues. The plane flew past the famed copper greeter, who held high her flame of liberty. They pressed their faces against the windows to catch a glimpse.

"I didn't know who or what the statue was," Danny recalled. "But there were people crying and there were people kissing and hugging because this giant statue was the symbol of America and of freedom, the virtue we all came here to find."

Whispering Danny and his family started life afresh in their new land. They found the needed medical attention, and except for the surgeries Danny needed every four months, life continued undisturbed. As Danny grew older, art became his passion and tattoos his medium. Danny opened a tattoo shop and lived the normal American life. Shane became his best friend, his drinking buddy. Rarely were they seen apart.

A roar approached the curb where Danny stood. Shane was riding his new motorcycle, enjoying the deep growls and the free air. Shane's eyes sparkled with the glee of his new grown-up toy. He slid off his helmet to the greeting of his friend.

"Shane, are we living right?" Danny asked.

"I was a cultural Jew," noted Danny, "not a religious one. I didn't disbelieve in God, but I couldn't say I knew anything about him. I started to have questions. Shane grew up in church, and I knew that when he was in high school, he was what he called a 'Bible thumper.' I wasn't entirely sure what that meant, but I figured he knew more about God than I did. So I asked him a very simple question."

Drinking defined their life and their friendship. The sordid culture of a tattoo shop and a neighborhood of bars marked their lives well. Danny knew his life wasn't right but couldn't really pin down what to change or how to change.

"There's a story of two sons who had a father," Shane began. His legs still straddled the bike; his helmet rested on his hip. His eyes saddened as he recalled a familiar story told by Jesus. "One of the sons decided to leave his home. He went to his father and asked for his inheritance. The father agreed. The son left the land of his birth and lived a life of squander. He spent his money on drinking parties and women and excessiveness.

"Then a famine struck the land," Shane continued. "Having spent all of his money, he lent himself out to feeding a bunch of swine. He was feeding those pigs and he thought to himself, *I would gladly eat the slop that I'm feeding these pigs, because I'm starving. But at my father's house, even the slaves eat better than this.* So the son decided to return home. As he approached home, his father saw him in the distance and began racing toward his returning son.

"'Father,' the son said. 'I've sinned against you. I've brought shame to the family. Let me come back into your household as a slave.'

"But the father was so overwhelmed by the joy of his son's return that he prepared a feast and showered him with gifts. He welcomed his erring son home with open arms.

"Now, I was even more confused," Danny admitted. "I had no idea why Shane told me this seemingly random story. I figured Shane had already begun our night of drinking a little early. So I ignored it. We walked into the bar, ordered our drinks, and thought nothing else of the story or my question."

They drank well past the warmth and the buzz of a casual drink, drinking themselves into a blind stupor. They drank and talked and laughed till midnight. Then Shane got a phone call. He got up to meet another friend at another bar.

"Don't do it, Shane," Danny begged. "You've had too much."

But Shane refused to listen. He pulled his motorcycle to a stand. He lifted his leg to mount the bike, but his drunken balance crashed them both to the ground. He brushed off the dust and tried again. Finally succeeding, he roared up the street, leaving Danny in his wake.

Danny downed the last of his drink and left the bar. Feeling an odd compulsion to go for a drive, he borrowed a car and wandered through the neighborhood. In the distance an object lay across the center. As he approached, it proved to be a motorcycle similar to his friend Shane's. Another twenty feet and there lay a man, sprawled across the center line. The street was dark except for a lone lamp glancing off a darkened pool of red that spread under the body.

Danny jumped out of the vehicle and saw it was Shane, lying facedown on the road. His helmet had rolled to the side and his head had broken open. He lay in a pool of dark, dark blood. Danny bent down on all fours and put his face next to Shane's, his cheeks warmed by the touch of his friend's blood.

"Shane, you're going to be okay," he told his friend. But Danny knew it was a lie.

They rushed him to the hospital and into emergency surgery.

"He's still alive," the doctor said, coming out of the operating room. "But he won't be for long. We had to take out a large portion of his front temporal lobe. It's the part of the brain that controls speech, hearing, eyesight, the ability to move, and a host of other functions. If by some slim chance he survives, he will never be the same."

The doctors labored to relieve the cranial swelling, but to no avail. Hope drained with each passing hour and with each passing day. Chances of survival narrowed to nothing.

"The good news was that he wouldn't be in this condition for long," Danny remembered. "He would quickly pass. So we sat and waited for Shane to die. I remember spending the night with Shane in the intensive care unit, trying to talk to him, but there was no one there. He was just an empty shell. Finally, somebody from the hospital came and spoke to the family about organ donation."

Shane's mother understood but asked for a final day to say her farewells. Just then a man walked into the lobby.

"I didn't know if he was a preacher or a priest or a pope," Danny said. "But there was something about this guy."

"Gather round. Gather round," he shouted. "We're going to have a prayer circle."

Well, Jewish people don't have prayer circles, Danny thought. *But I guess it can't hurt.*

"Oh God in heaven," the man prayed. His arms reached toward the ceiling and his voiced boomed down the corridor. "We have a situation here at St. Luke's Hospital. This young man, Shane, is so broken that no man on Earth can fix him. His brain has been busted and there's absolutely no way that he can recover. But God, we know you can fix him. So won't you please fix him? And by the way, we need him fixed before tomorrow morning. Amen."

"Amen," repeated the crowd, Whispering Danny along with them. It seemed like the right thing to do. He had never heard a prayer like that before. He went home running it through his head, examining each word and every phrase. But the more he analyzed it, the more disturbed he felt.

"I had participated in that prayer by saying, 'Amen.' But I didn't know anything about prayer or God or anything. So I started to ask all these questions. The first question I asked was, did I believe in God? That was an easy one. I believed God existed. He was up there somewhere and I was down here, minding my own business. I didn't really understand much about him. But there was enough going on in my life to recognize that there was a God. Then I asked myself if God could do this healing we had just asked for. It was impossible by any other means, but if God is who everyone says he is, then he could do anything. So this shouldn't be that big of a task for him to accomplish.

"I believed in God and I believed he could do what we asked him," Danny said. "But then I had to wonder why he would grant this favor. When you ask somebody for a favor, and I was asking for a big one, you don't ask a stranger. You always ask someone that you have a relationship with for a favor. I didn't have that relationship with God. So there I was asking for this grand request, a miracle really, and not just a miracle but one with a time restraint on it. We needed it to happen by tomorrow. I realized that I had no right to ask God for such a thing when we were not even friends.

"Well, that led to the next thing. If I'm going to ask God for such a great favor, we needed to become friends. That part scared me more than anything. If I was going to ask him for this big request, we couldn't be strangers. And that terrified me. I've never really been one to do things halfway. I knew that if I were to embark on a relationship with God, it would change my life forever. I liked my life. But I knew that this was the only way. But I didn't know how. I was Jewish. I really didn't know much about Christianity as a whole, but I knew that Jesus was involved and I remembered hearing the word *salvation*. So I Googled *Jesus* and *salvation*."

A Web site came up that asked a simple question. "Are you a sinner?"

It was never something he struggled with admitting. He always knew that he was a sinner. His life was never what it should be. Then the site instructed him to say a prayer. Before he prayed it, he read it through.

"It had some very interesting ideas in it. It talked about Jesus having died on the cross for me. It talked about how through his blood and his sacrifice, I was forgiven and that now I could be a part of God's family. But all this could only happen through what Jesus had done. I read it through a second time, but this time I prayed it as I went."

Then next morning began with a ring. A phone call woke him from his dreams with a hysterical voice on the other end.

"Shane woke up!" the voice stammered. Danny rushed over to the hospital and walked into Shane's room. Doctors and nurses were running around frantic, doctors yelling at nurses. Obviously they had the wrong CAT scan or the wrong MRI, because it was impossible for him to be awake because that part of his brain was gone. They were sending him off for further scans, but there he was wide awake.

"It's a miracle!" they kept saying.

Shane kept getting better and better, and in a couple days they had to kick him out of the intensive care unit. Danny asked him about the story Shane told the day of the crash.

"Why did you tell me that story, Shane?" Danny asked.

"I grew up a good Christian kid," Shane said. "I haven't been that person for years. You have never known that part of me. But I am that son. I walked away from God, my Father. But until I nearly lost my life on my motorcycle, I still hadn't returned home. I am at a point now where I am ready to return home."

"I never knew the Jesus part of Shane," Danny said. "I only knew the drinking buddy side. He didn't read his Bible or go to church or any of the things that I thought Christians did. I now claimed to believe in the same Jesus. I decided that I needed to learn more about Jesus."

Danny bought a Bible and began reading it. He read the section called "the Gospels." They told the story of Jesus' life and teaching. They detailed his sermons and his struggles, his death and his return to life.

"I felt like I was betraying my family, dishonoring those

that perished in the Holocaust, but I knew that this was truth. I started reading my Bible obsessively. I found it to be the most amazing book I'd ever encountered. No matter how many times I read it, it spoke to me about exactly what was going on in my life at the time. I've read a lot of books in my life, but I've never read one like this.

"I carried a burden for a long time about converting to Christianity from Judaism. But I realized I couldn't deny something that had revealed itself to be true to me. I am more certain of the reality of who Jesus is than I am certain of sitting in this chair right now. Jesus himself was a Jew. Jesus came into this world to draw the Jewish people as well as the non-Jewish people into a more intimate relationship with God the Father and himself. I certainly cannot have any ill feeling about that."

Danny struggled to discover his new purpose in life. He continued to paint tattoos on lost souls in a dark side of town. But he found those lost souls needed an ear to hear and a heart to care for them. Each customer who sat in his chair became a captive audience. He could speak truth into their lives, share his story, and offer his prayers. He could sit and listen to the pains and struggles of his fellow man and be a light where few lights shone.

"I started giving away Bibles," he said. "I bought them by the box. At first, I doubted whether people would appreciate my gesture, but they loved it. I've given away hundreds and never has anyone complained. I started inviting these people to a Bible study in my home. We started off with just a handful, but within a month, forty people filled my home. People were getting saved, lives were radically changed. It was a crazy beautiful thing.

"People sometimes ask why God allows bad things to

happen, like with Shane. I don't have those answers. I'm not qualified to understand why God does what he does. I don't know why bad things happen to good people. But I'm also incredibly underqualified to make the earth spin or to make the planets stay their orbit. I just have to accept those kinds of things by faith and trust God knows what he is doing.

"The thing about knowing Jesus personally is that suddenly a void is filled, and I've been able to know God in a way that's so much more relational than I ever thought possible. Through Jesus I can not only know God, but I can have real interaction with him. There is nothing else like it. It's not just religious stuff. It's having genuine interaction that goes both ways. I talk and I get answered. I get guidance. I get everything I need."

Watch the Film

Whispering Danny
Iamsecond.com/whisperingdanny

To see other stories like this, please visit:

Shane Kampe
Iamsecond.com/shanekampe

Anne Rice
Iamsecond.com/annerice

Skateboard Love

Brian Sumner

The dreary skies and downtown buzz of the Liverpool streets filled his senses. A thousand years of history rested beneath the brick-covered sidewalk. Shop windows stacked with modern trinkets, Beatles memories, and the paraphernalia of their local soccer heroes all called for his attention. But Brian's eyes caught something else. A kid, slightly older than he, glided along the crowded walkway. Few seemed to notice, fewer even cared, but Brian could look at nothing else.

His father walked beside him as Brian's pace slowed to a stop. Brian stared at this rocket shooting toward him. The boy stood on a skateboard, a piece of plywood inches above the ground, curved upward at both ends, screwed to four small wheels. The boy's shoes were aged and torn by the rigors of the street. His hair hung long and untrimmed. Baggy pants rode low over his feet, frayed at the end, betraying their constant use on this sailing plank of wood and wheels.

The boy flew by a man leaning against his unclaimed taxi. His knees bent low and arms spread slightly to his side. His feet inched back on the board and lunged upward, the board following close beneath. No straps, no holds, but the board tumbled through the air obeying its rider's every command. Freedom and confidence spread across the boy's face. The board clanked back to the ground, the boy landing atop its back and continuing his flight down the sidewalk.

"I had never seen anything like it," Brian said, remembering the moment he found his first love. "How does a skateboard jump? How does it tumble beneath his feet? I knew in that moment that that was what I wanted to do. I wanted to skate. A few months later I got my first skateboard.

"I grew up with this chaos around me. I was always angry. Liverpool was a rough place. I got into a lot of fights. People there handled everything with their fists. There was this song, 'You Will Never Walk Alone.' We always sang it at our soccer games. But as a kid I felt like I did walk alone. I felt like I was separate from everyone else. I didn't have a clue what life was all about. I grew up without vision or direction. I was looking for something to latch onto, something that could provide meaning for my life. Skateboarding became that thing."

Skating became his identity, his love. All his time was spent atop his board. He learned the tricks and wore the clothes. Brian became a regular on the streets of Liverpool. He soon began to enter and win skateboarding contests. By the time he was fifteen, he started receiving free product flow from some of the biggest skateboarding sponsors in the world.

"I tell people there are a lot of times in my life when I fell in love, but I really fell in love with skating. It defined me. Looking at the side of a skateboard, the plywood, seeing the trucks and the metal, the way the bearings rotated. Skating down the broken roads, ten in the morning to ten at night, skateboarding was who I was. Before skating, I didn't really have a life, I just existed. Skating brought me to life. It became my idol. My friends would ask if I could throw one thing off a bridge, would it be a girlfriend or my skateboard, I'd tell them she'd be swimming."

He chased his skating dreams to America when he was fifteen. He came to see how far he could take his skating. He moved to Southern California to a house on Warner Avenue. Brian Sumner, Aaron Reynolds, Jim Grecko, and other skating pros formed the Warner Avenue Crew.

Brian went pro by the time he was eighteen. He rode for Tony Hawk's skateboard company, Birdhouse. Besides the occasional phone call home, skating was all the responsibility he had. It was barbeques, parties, and Jacuzzis. Video premiers, photo ops, tours, and skating, it all became his life.

"I was living the dream. I could hardly believe that I skated for a living," he said. "It happened so fast.

"I never got in any serious kind of trouble," he said. "I knew that if I did I would be sent back to England. But the chaos seemed to be rumbling in the background. Friends started to get messed up on drugs or alcohol; an emptiness began to taint my accomplishments. The anger that plagued my younger years began to surface again. I started to get into more fights."

He fell in love at thirteen with skateboarding, and at nineteen with a girl. They were crazy, young, and in love. They thought the euphoria would never end. Every day was about love and passion. In a fit of youthful spontaneity, they ran off to Vegas and married in the first little chapel they saw.

"Up to that point, it was four months of passion, of loving each other. But it was a selfish kind of love. I loved her because of the way she looked or the way she treated me. She loved me because of the way I made her feel and because of that thrill inside her heart. But in the end, it was all about feeling good. It was selfish. We were just loving ourselves, really. Then we got pregnant."

They wanted a baby. They thought they were ready. The baby came and the attention went from love and passion to parenthood. The ease of young love faded with time and with new responsibilities. Brian traveled and toured and the money started to pour in, but the stress of everything began wearing on their relationship.

"I kept thinking that everything was about me. It was about how I felt and what I wanted. We fell in love because of the way we made each other feel. Now, the feelings were lost, the connection broken. And within a year and half of having our son, we're fighting like crazy. I'm punching holes through the walls, holes through windows, shouting and spitting and saying foul words to this woman I love."

He looked for meaning in skateboarding and he found it for a while, then it was love, but that, too, faded. Nothing seemed to last. An anger, a frustration about life boiled over into his marriage and his skating.

Where's the dream? he thought. "I came to America to find the American dream, and I found it, but I was miserable and angry. I accomplished more than I ever dreamed of doing. I had my face in magazines, my name on skateboards and T-shirts, but I felt so empty. I was full of anger. I said wicked things to my wife, things I didn't even believe, but I said them because I was so stupid and so mad. The anger was just boiling inside of me. Before we knew it we were divorced."

He couldn't understand why he wasn't happy, why he

wasn't satisfied. His friends medicated themselves with alcohol, drugs, and sex, with trying to be nice, with false hopes and false satisfaction, but it was all vain and temporary. He needed to find meaning and purpose. Was there a God? Did God care about Brian Sumner?

"I'd had enough fun," he said, "and it wasn't fun anymore. It was fun for a season. It was enjoyable for a moment, but now I needed answers.

"I grew up five doors down from a huge church with big green-brown walls and a gate. I'd go skateboarding there as a kid. I'd see the statue of Mary, the holy water. But I never knew anything about God. I never heard the message of Jesus. I walked around with no understanding about life. I looked at the church as something that people do. But why they went, the cross, Mary, the guy wearing a suit, none of it made any sense to me. But I was at a point now where I needed to search things out.

"I knew God was out there," he admitted. "But that was all I knew. Was it Buddha? Is he a Rasta? Was he in Ouija boards and séances? God was just this higher power. He was the guy at the pearly gates at the end of life."

But nothing was making any sense. He had his dreams. He skated all over the world. He married the girl he loved, but now it was all falling apart. He was empty and dissatisfied, frustrated and angry. Why couldn't he be happy? He searched, wondering if God was real, if he really cared.

"I couldn't control my anger. I got in more and more fights, got in trouble with the cops, got arrested and sentenced to community service."

Searching through community service opportunities, he stumbled across a Christian thrift store.

A Christian thrift store? he thought. *That'll be interesting. Christians are those crazy people who pray to a God they don't see. They always want your money and some of those priests mess with kids.*

That was all he really knew about Christians. Half out of curiosity, he signed up to work at the store. But the first day on the job he noticed a bookshelf, and on it was Lee Strobel's book *The Case for Christ*.

"At that point I was near suicidal. All I was doing was hating life and fighting with my ex-wife. I told God that I was going to prove that he wasn't real. In the back of my head, I really hoped he was real, but I couldn't see him. I was looking for something, for God really, but I didn't know it. This book was a journalist's investigation of the evidence for Jesus. I was going to read this book and prove it wrong. But I knew if there was no God, then everything was meaningless. If I was just a monkey, then nothing mattered, everything was permissible.

"I read everything. I read *The Case for Christ, Origin of Species*, the Bible, books on Rhastafarianism, Jehovah's Witnesses, Mormons, Hinduism, Buddhism, all the different 'isms' around the world. And I kept saying to God, 'Who's right in all of this? I don't have the answer and I need one. I need you to speak to me.'

"I wanted to know if this Jesus person was alive," he said.

Brian knew if Jesus was alive, if he was real, then that changed everything. Jesus was more than a philosophy or a moral code; he claimed to be the Son of God. If he was real, then Jesus had a real claim on his life.

"The world changed when a man called Jesus Christ lived. And Jesus claimed that someone like me, messed up and in need of help, could meet him, could really know him. I needed to know if that was true, if he could really change my life. I even talked with Christian Hosoi, a fellow skateboarding pro, who claimed to have had a real experience with Jesus. I asked him if he was real, if Jesus really changed his life. Christian said he did."

All his studying and questions brought him to a point where he believed. But he needed to know for sure. He needed to meet Jesus.

"I've never met you," he prayed. "I won't follow something that's fake. I won't make my life about something that's not real. I believe the Bible. I believe in Jesus, that he was a good man and more than that I believe he is God. But I've never met you. I need to meet you."

Brian sat in a dark corner of his room. The long shadows of his midnight prayers stretched across the floor. He cried to God, begging to be heard.

"I prayed for thirty or forty minutes," he said. "I got on my knees, asked him to forgive me of my sins, and begged him to let me meet him. As I cried out, I felt in an instant the craziest thing I can ever say in life. I felt a presence enter the room. I remembered this verse from the Bible that said, 'Draw near to God and he will draw near to you.' That is what I was doing, I was drawing near to God. And as I did that night, I felt the presence of God enter that room and in an instant—*boom*—the lights came on and I met God.

"I instantly began to cry," Brian said. "God is real. I couldn't believe that I had lived my whole life not knowing that God was real, that I could meet him. I couldn't believe that people didn't know this. My friends, family, so many people in my life didn't know that God was real. Now, I wanted everyone to know. God filled me that night. God spoke to my life. I told him right then that I would go around the world and tell everyone. Jesus Christ showed up that night and changed my life and filled me in a way that I can't explain. It began transforming everything about me. From that moment on, I've wanted everyone to know about God."

Brian changed after that night. The anger left. The frustration and emptiness were gone. His ex-wife noticed the difference and she, too, became a believer. They soon decided to remarry. They had begun attending church. And one night, with no planning and with all the reminiscence of their first spontaneous elopement, they showed up at their pastor's home and were married a second time.

"That night I looked at my wife without the feelings of frustration and anger I once had. I love her, not because she's my wife, but because she's God's daughter. I don't get mad at her because she falls short, because we are both God's children. Our marriage is proof of the love and grace and forgiveness of Jesus Christ."

"God gave me this gift for a reason," he says. "I can go to the skate park and use skating to reach people that another guy might not be able to. That's why I skate today. It's to tell people about Jesus.

"Am I still angry?" Brian said. "That's a crazy, crazy question. Wow. I'm not. I'm not angry. And it's all because of Jesus. Jesus is first. I am second, and I enjoy it."

Brian Sumner continues to skate professionally. But it's no longer about him. It's not about the money, the fun, or the pride of it. He skates for God.

Watch the Film

Brian Sumner
Iamsecond.com/briansumner

To see other stories like this, please visit:

Christian Hosoi
Iamsecond.com/christianhosoi

Lecrae
Iamsecond.com/lecrae

Faith and War

Chris Plekenpol

American forces invaded Iraq in the spring of 2003 when Saddam Hussein refused UN Inspectors who wanted to verify that he did not have weapons of mass destruction. Coalition Forces, led by the United States, toppled the government. The quick victory was short lived as insurgents began pouring over the borders and cropping up throughout the native soil. The real battle for Iraq had just begun. The Marines lost the city of Fallujah as thousands of insurgents forced them to evacuate an untenable position.

Chris Plekenpol was stationed in Korea, completing his final year of duty, when his commanding officer called him to his office. He had an offer to extend Chris's stay with the army for another year. "I want you to take command of your tank company," his colonel said. Chris would command fifty-five men and fourteen tanks. The offer proved tempting.

What's one more year? he thought. *It will be great leadership experience.* He took the command and immediately began training his men on the gunnery range twelve miles south of North Korea. However, Captain Plekenpol wouldn't be leading troops against Kim Jong II. His commander called him again only twelve days after taking command.

"I need you to make an assessment of your men. I can't tell you why, but you can probably figure it out." Later that night they gave him his orders. He was going to Iraq to patrol a major supply route connecting Fallujah to Ramadi, two terrorist hot spots.

"Two months later I am in the sandbox of Iraq. I'm commander of a hundred men, twenty-one tanks, seven Bradley Fighting Vehicles, and several Humvees."

Contact with the enemy would be an everyday occurrence there. Snipers, rocket propelled grenades (RPGs), and improvised explosive devices (IEDs) besieged this strip of rock and sand daily.

Heat waves bounced off the minarets. The blistering sun peaked at 120 degrees. A thousand hues of brown blanketed the ground and sky. Rock, dust, and trash littered the streets. Spots of green palms broke the tedium just south of the Euphrates River. This would be his first day of command in an active combat zone, and it would be a day forever burned in his memory.

"It seemed like a normal day. People were in the markets buying groceries. I stood outside my command post watching my tanks roll out into sector. We were supposed to take over the patrol at fourteen hundred hours."

He glanced down at his watch. He was four minutes into his first battlefield deployment.

Boom!

The earth quaked beneath him. Fire burst through the air a quarter mile ahead. The smoke curled into a two-hundred-foot mushroom in the sky. A brief moment of silent shock was broken by desperate radio calls. Emotion and chaos buzzed through the radio waves. Chris ran to his command post, trying to figure out what had happened. Situation reports flew across the radio. Men were talking all over each other. Gunfire and screams of pain echoed in the background. Then three letters echoed in his ears: K-I-A, killed in action; a man was dead. A soldier was lost.

Chris grabbed his rifle and 9mm pistol. He put his flack vest on as he sprinted to his tank. His crew spotted him running toward them and scrambled to ready the tank. Adrenaline rushed through their veins with the unwelcome onslaught of battle. A forty-five pound 120mm round was thrown into the breach of the main gun. The .50 caliber machine guns were charged and readied as the driver pushed the seventy-two-ton tank across base boundaries toward the engagement. As Chris exited the west gate of the forward operating base, another tank returned. The entire right side of the tank was decimated by the initial explosion. The sergeant who once commanded the tank was dead.

"Emotions were high. I just lost my first soldier and I was headed into my first fire fight. But I couldn't think about it right then."

Captain Plekenpol rushed to the battle and started taking small arms fire, machine gun fire, and mortars from the north side of the Euphrates. He ordered three tanks to pound the enemy and suppress their fire. Fifteen minutes of volleying bullets and mortars and the enemy began to withdraw to the north, overwhelmed by the American firepower. Chris sent two tanks to pursue them across the river. One hundred infantrymen began searching house to house for clues as to who was behind the attack. But in seven hours of searching, they found nothing.

"At the end of the day I was physically exhausted. The

scorching heat, fifty pounds of gear, running around for seven hours took its toll. Emotionally, I was a mess. I just lost my first soldier. I had to go back and write a letter to his wife and thirteen-year-old daughter and explain to them how I let their father and husband die. I had one job as a military commander, and that was to bring everybody home alive, and in the first four minutes on the job I failed."

Captain Plekenpol gathered his men that night and briefed them that this was their mission: For the next 364 days they would go out and put their lives on the line to defend Iraqi freedom. They would be shot at, bombed, attacked, killed, and maimed. They would fight an elusive enemy who would not be easily deterred. The reality of war had sunk in.

"I felt like God took the day off. Where was he when that sergeant was killed?"

Chris became a believer when he was twenty-two, but war has a way of testing faith.

"God and I had a deal," he said. "He told me that he would never leave me nor forsake me. That's what he promised in the Bible. But six years later I am in Iraq with a man dead and I feel like God abandoned me."

The first month was unrelenting. Every day, enemy fire, IEDs, and a rising insurgency barraged his company's sector. The heat wore on their patience. The constant threat of death beat on their souls. God seemed to fade into the background.

"I don't even feel like I'm a Christian at all," Chris wrote to his mentor back home. "I feel like I can't pray. I can't read my Bible. I'm struggling. I shouldn't even be writing this e-mail. I should just be praying or doing something spiritual, but I feel like I can't."

"Chris, you just rest," his mentor wrote back. "There's a

lot of people praying for you right now, standing in the gap while you are struggling. Just know that we are behind you one hundred percent."

Whether it was the prayer or knowing he had support back home, Chris found a new strength. He made a commitment, a decision to seek God. Every morning he would rise before the sun to spend an hour with God.

"The support back home was vital, but I knew I couldn't make it a whole year like that. There was no way I would be able to function leading that company for a year of combat if God didn't become a priority in my life."

The sun had yet to wake. The desert chill still hung in the morning air. He rolled out of bed and drove his Humvee across the silent base toward the chapel. He unfolded two metal chairs, one facing the other. "God, I'm lonely," he prayed. "I don't know what you are doing. I'm frustrated. I'm having a hard time seeing your plan in the midst of the chaos. I need you to sit with me, teach me, talk with me. This is our time."

He said, "I prayed everything I knew to pray; I laid it all out for him, but five minutes later I was done. I ran out of things to say. The next fifty-five minutes I spent staring at my watch, waiting for God to say something to me. I thought he was supposed to talk back. But I had made a commitment and this was what I was going to do. So I sat there and stared at my watch, journaled, read my Bible, and prayed some more."

Day after day he continued this spiritual exercise, fighting his heavy eyes and the ticking clock, searching for God.

"I found over time that I grew to love and cherish that time with God. It became the most powerful time of my day.

It translated later on to sensing God's presence in combat. I would pray and read my Bible and a certain peace came over me. It wasn't like I heard God come out of heaven and talk to me, but I felt like he spoke to me.

"God gave me a sense of peace. You always hear people talk about it in church. I always wondered what they were talking about. But for me God's peace meant that when I was out in sector I didn't feel like I was going to die. I didn't have that paranoia that death was knocking on my door. I had this peace that settled my soul. The peace gave me strength. There were a lot of tough decisions in combat. Sure, there were times where I was afraid or scared, but I was the commander. I had to be strong. I was carrying the weight of the whole company. His peace gave me the strength I needed."

He would indeed need that strength. The battle of Fallujah was mounting. American, Iraqi, and British troops massed around the city. Citizens evacuated. The insurgents dug in, fortifying their positions with IEDs, jury-rigged booby traps, and sniper positions throughout the city. More than two thousand insurgents guarded the city. On the night of November 8, 2004, the invasion began. Chris had sent one platoon (sixteen men, four tanks) to be part of the main support by fire effort. The rest of his company would maintain security between Fallujah and Ramadi. It seemed all of Iraq exploded and Fallujah was at the center. It would be the bloodiest battle of the war.

"We were in the middle of this campaign when a terrorist took a car stuffed full of bombs and plowed it into one of my men's tanks. We never saw him coming. It's not like terrorists wear uniforms. They look like everyone else."

The car crumpled against the massive seventy-two-ton

tank, but the bombs never exploded. The detonator was faulty or miscalibrated, or maybe the driver just didn't detonate the bomb in time. Whatever it was, something went wrong. The driver of the vehicle slammed his head against the steering wheel in the initial collision. His head was bloodied and his body limp. Chris moved his tank toward the car and saw the man still breathing. He wasn't dead. He never expected to survive past the initial hit, but he did.

"He was just sitting there with a car full of bombs passed out," Chris recalled. "I could see by the way that he was dressed that he was probably Syrian. He would be part of a whole network of terrorists. If I rescued him we might be able to get information vital to tracking down his fellow terrorists. But it would be a dangerous rescue."

He continued to peer into the smashed car from the safety of his tank. He saw the unharmed detonator resting in the front of the vehicle. If the man gained consciousness he could still attempt to detonate the bomb. Fearing the risk too great for a rescue, Chris called in Explosive Ordnance Disposal (EOD): the bomb squad.

EOD arrived and placed a C-4 charge on the detonator, attempting to blow the switch without blowing the bombs. The charge detonated and somehow caught the gas tank on fire. A blazing inferno erupted in the back of the car. The flames consumed and blackened the rear of the vehicle and slowly ate their way forward. The driver came to consciousness amidst the building heat. He opened the door and rolled out of the car, and then passed out. He woke up again when the flames came close to licking his scalp. He rolled away. But he couldn't stay conscious. Still within grasp of the impending explosion, he slipped out of consciousness. In and out of the waking world he fell, each conscious moment spent rolling away, trying to escape the inferno.

"There was a moment I could have saved him. I could've jumped down from my tank, run the hundred meters to the car, and carried him to safety. But what if he had a gun? What if he woke up and tried to fight me? I knew that if a struggle broke out we wouldn't be able to get back to cover. We would both die. I wasn't willing to die for my enemy. I wasn't willing. So I instructed my soldiers to stay clear of the car. No rescue was to be attempted. It was too dangerous. I didn't want anyone dying trying to save this man."

The flames licked forward, creeping closer and closer to the bombs. The man lay crawling in the street, fighting off death itself. He lifted his head searching for a brave soul willing to rescue an enemy. But no one came. The bomb exploded. The car shredded in the bombs' wake. The man's body took the full weight of the blast and tore under its force.

"The dust settled. I jumped off my tank and sprinted up to his body. A dark crimson painted the sand beneath him. I could have saved him, but I didn't. I was glad he was dead. He was my enemy. I wasn't willing to risk my life for a man sworn to kill me. But as I watched his life drain into the desert, a thought penetrated my heart.

"I, too, deserved death. I lived my whole life in open rebellion toward God. I never set off IEDs or rammed a car bomb into anybody's tank, but in God's eyes my rebellion still deserved death. Maybe I wasn't any worse than any other man, but neither was this terrorist any worse than any other terrorist. But death was still his just end. That was me. My sin deserved death.

"But Jesus took the penalty for me. While I was still a

sinner, still an enemy of God, Jesus came down, died on a cross, and shed his blood for me. He didn't sit back in his tank and watch me die. He didn't let my mistakes and my sins tear my body to shreds on some dusty God-forsaken street. He spilled his crimson blood instead of mine. He paid the price for me. He let me live when I deserved to die like a terrorist lying in the street.

"I'm not that kind of hero. Jesus did what I could never do. I'll die for my family. I'll die for my country, but only Jesus would die for an enemy."

The battle for Fallujah raged on for nearly two weeks, the longest sustained period of combat for US forces since Vietnam. Intermittent fighting continued through the next month. American forces sustained fifty-one deaths and more than four hundred seriously wounded. Enemy forces lost more than fifteen hundred fighters.

"God created this perfect order of things, and when our sin entered, it became a place of terror. Sin unchecked is a terrible thing. God exists in those moments to show us how desperately we need him, how he can redeem us, change us, give us new life. In combat you see that. There are places in life where God is an afterthought. You are driving down the road and life is pretty much all worked out, but in battle God is so much more real. I can't understand why he allows certain things to happen and I can't understand everything about God, but I guess that is what makes him God.

"I always come back to this one thought, life is so short. It's so urgent. I have this need to share the hope of Jesus with people who have no clue, who are still enemies of God. I want them to know that God took the hit for them. He has this irrational love for us, I just can't understand it. It doesn't make any sense to think that the Son of God would come down out of heaven and die a criminal's death for people that hate him. But he did it. He died for his enemies. He is crazy in love with his creation and he is willing to do anything to redeem us. And that is a message I want the whole world to know."

On August 6, 2006, Captain Chris Plekenpol resigned from the army to pursue full-time Christian ministry. His books *Faith in the Fog of War, Vol. I & II*, provide a powerful first-hand account of the Iraqi war and the faith that brought him through. Chris now travels as an ambassador for I am Second, spreading the message of God's love and the power of being second.

Watch the Film

Chris Plekenpol
Iamsecond.com/chrisplekenpol

To see other stories like this, please visit:

Tony Dungy
Iamsecond.com/tonydungy

Sujo John
Iamsecond.com/sujojohn

If Tomorrow Never Comes

Tamara Jolee

"My mom always tells the story of when I was five years old. She turned on the TV for me to watch cartoons, but all I wanted to do was read the newspaper. I never grew out of that. I loved hearing people's stories. I loved talking to people, connecting with people, telling their stories. I always knew that journalism wasn't about me. It was about reaching others and telling their stories.

"We all have battles to share, and I became a journalist to tell the story of those battles. Sometimes people say they don't have a story, that they are too ordinary. But that's never true. As a journalist I love being able to find that interesting aspect of someone's life. A story is your message, your testimony, your life. It's what the Lord speaks to you and through you even if you don't realize it."

Being a Christian and a journalist didn't mean she could get on TV and talk about Jesus every day. But it changed the way she approached her work. It was about more than getting the story or meeting the deadline. She was there to love people like God loved her.

"I would arrive on a murder scene and see utter brokenness," she said. "Someone is dead, a parent has lost a child, a husband his wife, and they need answers. I knew it was my job to do more than get the story. I would pray with them, love on them. I knew that this was what God wanted for my life. My faith has never been something that separates me from other people. It's a connecting point. I don't care about race, religion, or anything. I love people. That's the whole thing with God; he has taught me to love people no matter what.

"I was truly living my dream before it all happened. All my life I wanted to be a TV reporter. And finally, I got a job reporting for a major network. I was awarded my own television sports show."

Some doubted whether a woman could hold a thirty minute sports show, but the ratings shot up 200 percent after her arrival. She covered all the regional sports events, including the New Orleans Saints Super Bowl win that year. Life seemed perfect. Little did she know that everything was about to change forever.

It started with night sweats and irritated skin. But she wasn't worried. She figured it was stress or the environment. But it got worse. Sickness and fatigue became a regular battle. The tiredness turned to weight loss. Then the swelling began. Lymph nodes ballooned all over her body. She told herself it was an infection, that it would go away. But the swelling never left. Her lymph nodes bulged out more every day. "I could see them popping out of my legs," Tamara recalled.

"I finally went to the doctor," she said. "I knew something was wrong, but I never expected they would find what they did."

"Something's not normal," the doctor confirmed.

The doctor ran his tests. But the more he poked and prodded, tested and scanned, the quieter everyone became.

The doctor checked and rechecked his findings. Nurses scurried in and out of the room. A nervous silence descended on the staff. They avoided her look, evaded her questions.

"One hundred and forty-seven," they kept saying. They were shocked by the number.

"You have 147 swollen lymph nodes," they repeated.

She didn't know what that meant, but she could tell from their dodgy eyes and shaken voices that something was wrong.

"I wanted to approach things head-on," she said. "I wanted to see what was inside of me. I wanted to see exactly what I was facing. I asked over and over for details, but nobody would tell me. Until finally, the doctor sat me down and told me the news."

"We're not sure yet, but there is a chance you have cancer, a good chance," he finally told her.

"I still didn't believe it," she said. "His words went right past me. He said that there were more tests he wanted to run, but I was sure that it was all a mistake."

Early the next day, the deep Texas blue stretched across the sky. Tamara and her mother sat at home talking and laughing, thinking nothing of the tests. Then Tamara's phone rang. It was the doctor.

"I assumed he had good news," she said. "It was late in the week and I thought he was calling so I wouldn't have to worry about it over the weekend. I had convinced myself that everything was still fine."

"Hello," she answered.

There was a pause at the other end. The doctor hesitated. Tamara's breath fell short. A quiet fear built in her stomach. She began to fear the worst, that she wouldn't like what the doctor had to say. The reality of the moment started to take effect.

"Tamara," he finally said. She sat down, weakened with expectation, her mother close to her side.

"I don't know how to tell you this, but you have cancer, blood cancer," he said. "It's called Non-Hodgkin's Lymphoma."

She could hardly believe it. She sensed her mother's angst and fought to keep the smile on her face.

"And not only do you have cancer," the doctor continued, "it's all over your body. It's advanced stage four cancer, from head to toe. And there is no cure. People don't usually live more than five years with this kind of cancer."

Shock spread across Tamara's face.

"My first thought wasn't even about me; it was about my family. My mom lost both her parents to cancer. My grandfather died of the exact same thing I now had. I couldn't even talk. My whole body went into shock. How do I tell them? How in the world do I talk to my father, my mother, my brother and sister, and tell them that I'm dying?"

Her mother watched Tamara melt into the couch. She dropped the phone to her side. The blood drained from her face. Her mouth hung open, dry and paralyzed. She leaned forward, searching for a notebook. Tearing out a piece of paper, Tamara wrote three simple words:

"I have cancer."

Tamara grew up going to church and hearing about Jesus. She heard people talk about having a personal relationship with God, but it never made sense. How could someone personally know God?

"I wondered what all this God stuff was really about,"

she said, thinking back to her childhood. "I believed in God, but people talked about him like he was their best friend, like they just went out to lunch with him. I didn't understand what they were talking about."

She went to college and started looking for answers. Life had an emptiness to it. She tried partying. She tried love. She tried a career. But nothing filled the hole.

"I finally realized that God wanted more than my religious commitment; he wanted me. He wanted to sit next to me in class, to walk with me through life. God wanted to be my friend. Life was different after I realized that God wanted a relationship. He brought a sense of happiness to my life. I had my ups and downs of course, but it was different with God. I knew that no matter what, I was saved and I was loved. There were still battles to face, but having a relationship with God meant that there was always someone to lean on. When I found I had cancer, God was the first person I ran to."

Shock describes it best. She didn't fear death or question God. She just couldn't believe that she was going to die. She knew it would come one day, but never thought it might be so soon.

"But there was this peace that came over me. I never heard God say I was going to be healed or anything, but I knew that in some way he was going to be with me through it all.

"I'm not just living anymore," she said. "I'm surviving. I track everything, what I eat, how I carry myself. I try to make sure everything is in tune physically. People tell me now, 'Wow! You are doing so well.' But they weren't with me during the sleepless nights, with medical steroids roaring through my system. They didn't witness the vomiting and nausea caused by the chemotherapy. I was sick, real sick."

For eight hours she would sit in a sterile hospital room watching as the chemicals tore through her veins. She sat in her bed seeing the sunken eyes of fellow chemo patients sharing the room. So many lost hope, crushed beneath the inevitability of suffering and pain. The drugs were designed to save life, but they couldn't distinguish between cancer cells and healthy cells. The result was a pain hard to endure, nausea, hair loss, debilitating fatigue.

"Lord, I don't even have anything to say right now," she prayed so often in that room. "Just hold me, comfort me."

Every four months she fought through another round of chemotherapy. Her cancer can't be cured. She is only fighting for time—time to continue life, to continue the fight. But the day will come when the cancer will win.

"But I have a peace about it. I feel a sense of joy. I know this fight will continue from now until I die, but I know that God will be with me through everything. I often ask myself, 'Is it worth it? Is all this pain and fighting and chemotherapy worth the few years I might be able add on to my life?' But I always say yes. I hear God telling me to keep fighting, to keep going. I know he has more for me to do.

"In my eyes, getting cancer was the best thing that ever happened in my life. I know for a fact that I'm not living for myself. I'm living for God. Over and over I hear him speak to me. He wants me to share my story, to reach people, to bring encouragement and peace. That is what he has for my life, and that's worth all the chemo in the world.

"I have cancer in 90 percent of my body," she said. "I never know if tomorrow will be my last. But if I do die tomorrow, or even if I die today, I'm completely and truly at peace with that. I know I'm not alone."

"It's still all over your body," the doctor said. Every three months Tamara went in for another CT scan, but every scan was the same.

"For some reason the treatments aren't working," the doctor said.

She knew that her cancer was incurable, but her doctors hoped that chemotherapy would slow the inevitable. But with each scan, hope dissipated as the cancer showed no signs of regression.

The doctors had one last hope, a PET scan. The scan would be able to perform a deeper scan and hopefully better enable her doctors to design a successful treatment plan. Her last CT scan revealed the same dismal results, but with the help of this scan they hoped for better results.

"I no longer let my family come with me for my scans," she admitted. "I wanted to shield them. No one knew that the treatments weren't working. I would tell them things were going well because it was hard for them, but they weren't going well. My mother begged me to let her come with me to my PET scan. I finally relented."

A month later the doctor called with the results.

"Come on in and we can take a look together," the doctor said. "I haven't actually looked at them yet, but I will pick them up from the pathologist as soon as you get here."

She and her mother thought little of cancer or scans or chemotherapy except on days like this. Tamara walked through the door and sat down in the waiting room. She looked around the place where cancer weighed on everyone's mind. Hope rarely visited this room. They, like her, didn't like to think about the deadly cells growing inside their bodies, but in this room cancer was in everyone's thoughts.

"Your wait might be a little longer than usual," the nurse said as she brought Tamara and her mother to the back. "The doctor wanted to talk with you."

Her heart dropped. She thought the worst. There were only so many things he could want to talk about, and none of them seemed good. The next ten minutes seemed the longest of her life. The doctor walked in, his face white, his expression flustered, his eyes never leaving the file in front of him.

"Tamara, I just can't explain it," he said.

"Explain what?" she cried.

"It's not there," he admitted. "Nothing at all. I can't explain it. There is simply no medical explanation. Not one single lymphoma cell showed up on the PET scan. And it's the strongest scan we got. There is absolutely no medical evidence of your cancer. When the pathologist gave it to me, I had to consult with another doctor to make sure. I can't figure it out, but your incurable cancer is in remission."

"My mother never shows emotion," Tamara said. "We are both solid rocks when it comes to crying, but she was weeping by this point. We both were. It was a miracle. So many people have prayed. So many people have cried. And now I was healed."

"I was at peace with dying. I came to the point where I was glad I had cancer. It taught me about God. It let me understand the suffering so many families face with cancer. It gave me a voice and story to share, but now God has given me a new life."

Tamara Jolee's cancer is officially in remission. Her cancer is still considered incurable, and so her doctors warn that it will likely return. But her story is not about healing. It's about faith and suffering. It's about Tamara learning to walk with God through the dark hours of her life. She learned that whether or not someone is healed from cancer, God is there.

Watch the Film

Tamara Jolee
Iamsecond.com/tamarajolee

To see other stories like this, please visit:

Janelle Hail
Iamsecond.com/janellehail

Mike Huckabee
Iamsecond.com/mikehuckabee

Brian Birdwell
Iamsecond.com/brianbirdwell

Death and
Football

Bradie James

Something was special about the Cajun atmo-sphere in the Louisiana fall. Students, families, and friends gathered early before football games to tailgate: enjoying the spicy jambalaya, crawfish, shrimp, and red beans and rice.

Bradie, one of the players, had a gift and the work ethic to become not just a great athlete, but one of the best in his state. On Sundays, ever since Bradie could remember, he went to church with his parents. Bradie learned the Bible at children's programs and youth group, and he sat though many long sermons. But he didn't fully understand every-thing he heard.

"I knew the verse that said, 'Consider it pure joy when-ever you face trials of many kinds, because you know that the testing of your faith develops perseverance.' But at the same time, I thought to myself, *Successful people don't really go through trials.*"

Bradie had his heart set on football success, and college coaches soon began recognizing his talent and recruiting him. That was when his father became seriously ill. As his father's health declined, Bradie's conversations with him turned more serious.

"Bradie, I'm thankful that you're making good grades,"

his father said. "But I need to talk with you about something deeper. If anything ever happens to me, Bradie, make sure that you take care of your mom."

Bradie listened carefully to his father's words. He graduated high school and received a scholarship to play football for Louisiana State University (LSU). His father was proud of him but knew he wouldn't be around much longer to guide him through life.

"As those conversations between my father and I started changing, I started thinking more seriously and maturing a little faster. My father passed away right as we were getting ready to play in the Peach Bowl, my freshman year. I decided to play the game anyways, because I knew that football was something my father really loved. So I went out there and dedicated the game to him. And I knew he would be smiling down."

Many of Bradie's friends didn't have a father. But Bradie's had been determined to raise his son well and teach him the value of family. They had a close relationship, and his death cut deep in Bradie's heart.

"My father was the reason I played football," Bradie said. "When he got sick, I was devastated. It was tough seeing that he couldn't be as active as he had been before."

His father wanted him to take care of his mother after he died. But shortly after Bradie's father passed away, Bradie's mother was diagnosed with breast cancer. Breast cancer was new to his family. He didn't know anything about it. He was still in college and his mother lived in another part of the state, but he did his best to take care of her.

"My family didn't tell me right away when she got breast cancer," he said. "I think they were trying to protect me, I had just lost my dad and was trying to make it through college. But when I finally found out, I wanted to learn everything I could about the disease."

Her cancer became aggressive and she was forced to go through chemotherapy to combat it. Bradie's whole family stepped in to help. His aunt and uncle lived nearby and did their best to help her through the process.

"It was tough," he said. "Everyone was doing the best they could, but our family just didn't know a whole lot about breast cancer. It was hard to see her go through it all."

One day, Bradie felt like he had to go home. He couldn't explain why, but he knew he needed to be with his mom. His brother felt the same and drove in from Dallas.

"We both happened to pull up at the same time," Bradie recalled. "We both just felt like something was wrong. I had asked my coach if I could go home for the weekend and he agreed. So that is what I did."

She died shortly after they arrived. Both of Bradie's parents were now gone. He didn't know what to do.

"I remembered the verse again that said, 'Consider it pure joy whenever you face trials of many kinds, because you know that the testing of your faith develops perseverance.' I realized that verse was true. Everyone really does have to go through trials. My faith was shaken. I had mixed emotions. I felt if God was so sovereign and so good, how could he let these people that I loved so much leave? I wanted to trust God, but it was hard. My parents were my rock. They were always there when I needed advice, no matter what I was going through. Now they were gone."

Two years later, as team captain for LSU, Bradie was drafted into the NFL by the Dallas Cowboys. He graduated from LSU as a National Scholar Athlete. He had promised his family that he would graduate for his mom and dad.

"When I graduated, it was a joyous occasion," Bradie said. "It was a big deal for me to keep the promise I made to my family. But when I got drafted to the NFL, I felt like I still had this emptiness. Soon after that, I started to go to church again. It had been two years since my mom passed away, and I had been running from God. I was out having fun, living for the world. It was all about who had the biggest ego, the fanciest car, or the sweetest house. But at the end of the day, there was still that void.

"I met a woman who helped me understand love," he said. "Jesus had all this power when he walked the earth. He performed miracles. He fed the hungry. He healed the sick and raised the dead. But he still made the sacrifice and died on the cross for us. I could never really connect with that love until I found my wife.

"I always kept a distance from people," he said. "I was close to my parents and I lost them. I didn't want that to happen again. I felt like it was just better to be detached. I never let people really get to know me. My wife helped change that. I've realized through her that love is a sacrificial thing. The kind of love that Jesus had for me made him die on a cross. His love was sacrificial and that is the kind of love he wants me to have.

"That's what it means to be second. It's sacrificial love. My parents loved me. They always stayed together. If they wouldn't have stayed together, I don't know what I would be doing. Seeing them adhere to their vows gave me hope. Even through their death, I have learned about God. God never leaves. Even when the people you love die, God is still there."

Bradie James still plays football as a crucial member of the Dallas Cowboys. He has since established Foundation 56, an organization aimed at fighting the cancer that killed his mother.

Watch the Film

Bradie James
Iamsecond.com/bradiejames

To see other stories like this, please visit:

John Meador
Iamsecond.com/johnmeador

Daniel Sepulveda
Iamsecond.com/danielsepulveda

Greg Ellis
Iamsecond.com/gregellis

Surfing with Sharks

Bethany Hamilton

Her sun-bleached hair dripped with the sea. Volcanic mountains covered in green jutted into the sky behind her. Her board stood in the powdered Hawaiian sand by her side. She gazed at the crested sea that spread before her as she reflected on the wave that changed everything.

Hawaii is world renowned as a surfer's paradise. Warm waters with waves curling to foamy perfection surround the remote Pacific island chain. It is home to some of the world's best surfing competitions. Bethany has surfed these waves since she was five years old. She possessed an unusual talent for surfing and a love for these blue waters. She entered and won her first competition at the age of eight. Her love of the ocean soon brought her to top amateur competitions at a young age. She dreamed of reaching the professional level.

"There is something so special about surfing," Bethany said with a gaze that said she was riding a wave somewhere in her mind. "The feelings you get when you're on a good wave. The sun is just rising. The weather is perfect. The water is crystal clear and blue. My adrenaline is pumping and the blood is just flowing through my body. Every wave is different. To be out in the ocean in God's creation is a true gift, a true joy."

At thirteen, her young career seemed promising. Every day started before the sun took to the skies, before most kids were up for school. Her father was scheduled for knee surgery this particular morning. Bethany would be surfing with friends. Her mother drove her to the beach. They pulled up. Bethany threw open the door, jumped from the car, and listened for the surf.

"The surf is junk," Bethany called back to her mother. The waves were lower than she had hoped, but it didn't matter. She always welcomed a day at the beach, surfing the waves with her friends. Her mother smiled as Bethany and her friend Alana ran toward the water with their surfboards under their arms. Sand flung into the air as they ran. Their toes touched the warm waters as the first streaks of purple and orange spread through the sky. Alana's brother, Byron, and Alana's father, Holt, followed quickly after them.

The sun brightened as the morning passed. Bethany paddled out past the other surfers enjoying the serenity of the deep blue on a fresh morning. The sun warmed her back and the salt filled her pores. Her board skimmed the top of the water as her arms pulled her further out.

Suddenly, something caught her eye. A movement in the water rushed toward her. Before she could react, a shadowy grey mass grabbed her left arm from beneath the water. The shark shook his head back and forth, punching a hole in the board and severing Bethany's arm just past the shoulder. The pain of the gruesome wound deadened with the onset of shock. The fourteen-foot tiger shark disappeared as quickly as it came. Bethany made several feint strokes in the bloodied water toward her friends.

"A shark attacked me," she called to them.

Her voice was weak and serious. Bethany knew she needed to get to shore to survive. She didn't have time to wonder if the shark would attack again. Holt and Byron raced toward her voice. They grabbed her board, tied the surfboard leash around her shoulder to minimize bleeding, and quickly swam ashore.

"God, I'm in your hands," Bethany whispered. She felt cold. Her blood hemorrhaged into the waves as Holt pulled her to shore.

"Hold on!" Holt said, trying to keep her conscious.

I might die, she thought. "But I'm yours God. I'm yours," she whispered as she was dragged through the waves. They climbed ashore and called an ambulance. It rushed to the scene. Paramedics sprang from the vehicle and raced to meet Bethany lying in the sand. They loaded her onto a stretcher and carried her to the van.

"God will never leave you nor forsake you," one of the paramedics whispered into her ear as they pushed her stretcher into the back. Bethany gained fresh hope from the words. She knew it was true. It was hard to see in the moment, but she held onto hope. The ride to the hospital blurred as shock and blood loss dampened her senses.

The ambulance arrived at the hospital. Bethany's father, Tom, was being prepped for knee surgery. He had just received the anesthetic when a nurse burst into the operating room.

"Dr. Rovinsky," the nurse interrupted, addressing the surgeon. "A thirteen-year-old girl has just been attacked by a shark. We need this room for emergency surgery. They are bringing her up now."

It can't be! her father thought. Fear crept into Tom's head. But somehow he knew that thirteen-year-old girl was his daughter. He tried to get up but he couldn't. The anesthetic numbed his legs. He struggled to move, but his legs refused to obey. The doctor grabbed his things and began readying the room for the incoming patient.

"Calm down, Tom," Dr. Rovinksy said. "I'm going to check on this. Stay put. I'll be right back."

Minutes later, the doctor returned.

"Tom, it's your daughter. She is in stable condition. That's all I know right now."

Bethany's left arm was completely severed by the shark. By the time doctors were able to stop the bleeding, she had lost 60 percent of her blood. But with the quick response of her fellow surfers and the skill of the doctors, her life was spared.

Bethany thought back to those moments when death came so near.

"It goes through the mind of every surfer," she said. "You think how crazy it would be for a shark to attack you, but you don't ever really think it will happen to you. So I've never really been scared of sharks. I never thought it would happen. But when it did happen, I think being able to turn to Jesus is what kept me alive. He gave me a sense of peace and calmness. I just stayed calm and trusted in him during the whole thing. I remember just lying there and praying the whole way in, asking God for help. And he did. He helped me through it.

"I gave my heart to Jesus when I was five years old. It was never something my parents forced on me. I actually did it with one of my best friends. But ever since that day, Jesus has been a part of my life. It's a personal relationship. I talk to him every day. He is the one that I can come to at any moment."

After the shark attack Bethany didn't know if she would be able to surf again, but everything in her wanted to get back on her board. She wanted to fight back. She wanted to feel the spray of the waves and the board under her feet. Within a week of the attack, she asked her doctor to let her back into the ocean.

"I knew I wanted to continue surfing," she recalled. "But I had to wait on the doctor's orders to let me get back in the water. He told me I had to wait until I got my stitches out. I hated waiting. My biggest fear wasn't the sharks, it was not knowing whether or not I could still surf."

It was the day before Thanksgiving. Less than four weeks after the shark attack. Her doctor told her she couldn't surf for at least another day. Bethany and her friends went out to the beach. She sat on the shore watching them surf.

"I can't handle this," she said.

She needed to know if she could still surf. She got out her board and walked toward the water. Her feet hit the edge and paused. She felt the salt wash over her toes and the water curve around her ankles. A huge grin came over her face. She took another step deeper into the blue. Her board dipped into the rising water. And then she threw herself into the water, climbed on her board, and paddled toward the crashing waves.

She saw a wave rising from the ocean floor. She paddled back to catch it. She jumped to her feet with her board underneath. Her feet gripped for a moment but then she tumbled into the wave.

Another wave came. She swam to catch it. A thought came to her head, *What if I can't do this? What if I can never surf again?*

A stiff resolve filled her muscles. Her mind focused. She

saw in the distance another wave rolling up from the ocean floor. She paddled with all her might, racing the wave into the coast. Just as the wave began to rise, she stabled herself with her hand in the center of the board, she pushed up, and climbed to her feet. Her board skimmed across the side of the wave all the way to the beach.

"Right then I knew I would be surfing for a long time," she said with a smile beaming on her face.

"From what seems like such a horrible thing, God has been able to bring glory to himself through me. I've been able to be a light to people and share his love. I wake up every day and honor God in everything that I do. I may fall short sometimes, but all I want to do is love him.

"I don't think of Jesus as a religion. It's a relationship. He calls us to love him and to love others before ourselves. He calls us to put ourselves second. When we spend so much time in life living for ourselves, trying to make ourselves more well known, trying to make our own lives better, it's like running on a treadmill. When we put God first and others before ourselves, life is just a lot more exciting."

Bethany Hamilton returned to competitive surfing just two months later in January of 2004. She took fifth place in the open women's division of the National Scholastic Surfing Association (NSSA) tournament in Kailua-Kona, Hawaii. A year later she won her first national title at the 2005 NSSA National Championships. She turned pro in 2007, realizing a childhood dream. In 2009 Bethany launched Friends of Bethany, a nonprofit organization dedicated to sharing the hope and love of Jesus worldwide by supporting and encouraging shark attack survivors and traumatic amputees. Her autobiography, *Soul Surfer*, became a *New York Times* best seller and inspired the making of a major motion picture, which released in 2011 starring AnnaSophia Robb, Dennis Quaid, and Helen Hunt.

Watch the Film

Bethany Hamilton
Iamsecond.com/bethanyhamilton

To see other stories like this, please visit:

Lee Lucas
Iamsecond.com/leelucas

Brant Hansen
Iamsecond.com/branthansen

Riding with
a Mask

Laura Klock

Laura Klock grew up among the green fields and
rolling hills of rural Wisconsin. She learned early that her
motorcycle was her escape, the place where she could sing,
laugh, cry, and scream—and nobody cared.

"On my motorcycle, I felt like I was in control when the
rest of my life seemed out of control," she said. "I thought it was
my fault that my parents fought, that my dad drank. They did
their best, but there was a lot of chaos growing up. They were
young when they had me. I wasn't planned. I thought I wasn't
wanted. I thought if I did better in school, better in sports, better at whatever I did, that my parents would be happy."

So she wore a mask. She kept her pain hidden, never
wanting to burden anyone else, especially her parents, with
the hurt inside of her. She made it her responsibility to make
everyone happy.

"I discovered that when I drank I became more fun," she
said. "I came out of my shell. I learned that with alcohol I could
be this other person, the person I really was on the inside but
couldn't tell anyone. I didn't understand that I could just be
that person without adding alcohol.

"I started living a completely double life at a really young
age," she admitted.

On the outside, she excelled in school, played basketball, was a cheerleader and a good kid. But her mask covered the turmoil boiling on the inside. At the age of sixteen, she got pregnant. With no support and no information, she had an abortion. Her mom never knew.

"I saw the baby. I don't think I was supposed to, but I did," she said with that horrifying image crossing her mind. "I started to cry. The doctor came in and asked if I was crying because I was in pain or crying because I was a woman. I didn't know what to say. None of it made any sense. I carried with me the guilt and shame of that moment for years.

"I never felt good enough. Never quite pretty enough. Never smart enough. I tried to fill my emptiness with alcohol and then drugs. I tried work, accomplishments, relationships, but nothing ever filled it. I never felt any better about myself."

At twenty-one she gave birth to a baby girl and married the father. The whole relationship was built on partying, alcohol, and drugs. They had another child but the cycle continued. They would drop the children off with their grandparents for the weekend and then binge drink until Monday.

"On the outside, it looked like my life was all together," she said. "I had a family, a good job. I seemed happy, but my life was a mess. I would show up to work with cuts and bruises on my arms. People would ask me about them, but I would tell them that I fell down the stairs. My relationship with my husband was really dysfunctional, to say the least. Nobody knew there was a problem."

The marriage ended in divorce. She worked hard, took care of her daughters, and always tried to teach them all the right things.

"But I always hoped they wouldn't see the other side of me, the mess I tried to hide. Managing a double life was exhausting. It started when I was young, hiding things from my parents, but I never grew out of it. When I became a mom, it grew harder and harder to hide. My kids would see me drunk once in a while, see me making bad choices. I started to lose control over keeping my two lives separate."

She remarried. But still suffering with her low self-esteem and self-worth, the marriage crumbled around her. It, too, ended in divorce. She started a new relationship with another man, but he died suddenly from a heart attack soon thereafter. She sent her kids to stay with family and began a search for answers.

"I got on my motorcycle and just rode for days and days. I went to a lot of those dark places in my soul, looking for answers, trying to figure out why my life was such a mess."

She rode until she found herself in a small town in South Dakota. Brian, an old friend of hers, owned a shop there. She stopped by just to visit. But he needed help around the shop, someone to help organize the marketing and daily operational activities of the business. He had been praying for help when Laura walked through the door.

"My visit started sounding like a job interview by the end of the day," she recalled.

She agreed to stay on for a couple of weeks, but the weeks turned into months. She never left. Laura and the kids ended up moving to this small town in South Dakota. Brian invited her to come to church with him.

"My grandmothers were both godly women," she said. "They prayed for us. My parents would drop us off at Sunday school. But I didn't understand any of it. It was never modeled to me at home. I tried church when I was older but never had a good experience. When Brian invited me to go to church with him, I decided to go but I wasn't optimistic. Maybe because of where I was in life, I don't know, but this time it connected. It made sense. I started to find some of those answers I was looking for. I dove in. I got into every Bible study group they had. I joined a Celebrate Recovery group, a Christ-centered recovery program, and started down the path of healing."

But it was a long road. She and Brian started dating. She worked full-time at his shop and made South Dakota home. The relationship started to progress, and some of her old patterns began to resurface.

"Brian and I got in a fight. It was too familiar, too real and raw, too much like every relationship and every situation I'd been in all over again."

She went home and took a shower. She came out with her hair still wet and collapsed on the living room floor. It was happening again. It was a different house and a different state, but the relationship was going to the same place. She cried out to God.

"I'm here again," she prayed. "I'm in the same place all over again. I can't do it anymore. I can't run anymore. I can't. You can have it. Do with me whatever you want, because I give up. I surrender."

"I'd like to say that heaven opened up and the lights came down," she said. "None of that happened. But I did have a real experience. I felt a sense of peace. I realized at that moment that I wasn't in control. God was in control. And I had to let him carry my burdens, my worries, and my troubles. I'd been learning in my Celebrate Recovery group that God had a plan for my life, that I wasn't a mistake. God began to fill all of those empty holes in my life with his love and forgiveness, mercy and grace."

Around the same time, the Discovery Channel asked Brian and Laura to build a bike for their show *Biker Build Off*. They decided as a marketing move that they should race it. Laura had never raced before, but she decided to race the bike she helped build.

"I ended up on the starting line of the Bonneville Salt Flats," Laura recalled. "I prayed; I was just learning how to pray, and I said, 'God, this is where you have me today. Let me do your will.'"

She felt the rolling heat curling off the salted plain, the dry wind flowing through her hair. She thought back to all the twisted roads that led her to that place: the broken relationships, the partying, and all the masks she wore. And through it all, her bike was always something she had, a gift that God seemed to give her. But now she had a chance to use her gift for something greater than herself.

The current record in her class was 137.1 miles per hour. On her first pass she went 137.5. On the second pass she went 142 miles per hour, setting a land speed world record. Over the next several years, both her daughters captured their own records. Laura and her two daughters became the first mother-daughter-daughter trio in history to hold records at the same time.

"For me, the core issue was just an incredibly low self-worth. I thought accomplishments would make me feel better, but they never did. I held a lot of guilt about the abortion I had when I was sixteen and about all the failed relationships in my life. But God has taught me that he has a plan, that he loves me, that I have worth. It was when I surrendered, stopped trying to earn my worth, and just accepted what he was giving me that I started to find healing. I realized that day on the Bonneville Salt Flats that this record was not about earning worth but about an opportunity to share with people what God has done in my life.

"I thought that time would heal my wounds, but it didn't," she confessed. "I had to face them. I had to take off the mask and face the truth. I don't feel worthless anymore. I wake up excited every day, because I know God is in control. I am still in process. But he is filling the holes in my life. Brian and I are now married. In a lot of ways it's been the toughest of all my marriages, but we have a foundation to stand on. I feel that no matter what happens, God will bring us through."

Watch the Film

Laura Klock
Iamsecond.com/lauraklock

To see other stories like this, please visit:

Janine Turner
Iamsecond.com/janineturner

Gridiron Battles

Sam Bradford

A helmet weighs on his head. Pads press across his shoulders. Sweat wets his face and runs down his back; his nostrils breathe in the adrenaline-laced sweat of his teammates. He scans the thousands of cheering fans. The grass and dirt of a virgin field ready for a new season lies before his eyes. His feet have trod hundreds of similar scenes. Pads, turf, a crowd, and a leather ball. But this one is different. This field invites only the finest human machines to battle the gridiron foes. This is the NFL. Many dream of this opportunity, but few cross the white painted line to enter its battle. Today, Sam Bradford will be one of those few.

The whistle blows. He lifts his foot and leans forward. A thousand moments flash across his mind. The first touch of the ball's leather and lace. The first pass to a ready receiver. The football soaring through the air and landing in the chest of a fellow athlete. From a child playing in his backyard to high school hero to college football's most decorated player of the year, it has all led him to this moment when he is crossing the white line into the dream that is the NFL.

He jogs out to the huddle. The stadium roars with enthusiasm. His stomach tightens and his lungs shorten with the pressure of his first play. It never changes. The nerves never leave. Questions fill his head.

Will I play well today? he thinks. *Are we prepared? What will the defense throw at us? How will we respond?*

But as soon as the huddle forms, the world dies away. The crowd's roar falls deaf on his ears. It's just him, the ball, and his target. This is when the early morning workouts, the afternoon drills, the late night film room all pay off. He didn't just show up today. He has studied this team, their defense, their weaknesses, their tendencies. He knows when they blitz and when they fall back. He knows the speed of his receivers, their turns, and their fakes. He knows where they will be when the ball smacks them in the chest. For him, this is more than just a game. It's a battle. But he doesn't fight it alone.

"Everybody puts a lot of pressure on me to play well. I put a lot of pressure on myself. I know that if we lose a game or I play poorly, there are going to be a lot of people upset with me. I know that I'm going to be upset with myself. But I realize I'm not doing it by myself. Obviously I have teammates and we work as a team, but I know there is something more than that. I know God is out there with me.

"Having a relationship with God allows me to get away from everything else," he says. "When I'm with him, I stop thinking about football. I stop thinking about my problems. Everyone has their battles. But without God we are in those battles alone. We face impossible opponents; we're outmatched. Without God we don't have a chance to win. But with God it's different."

His dad taught him to love the game, but he also taught him the value of hard work. He taught him that it wasn't about beating the other guy; it was about playing his best, about competing against himself.

"I take that to heart," Sam says. "I expect to be my best in everything. Whether it's on the field or in the classroom, or just playing ping-pong in the garage, I expect to win. Sometimes I am tempted to doubt God when I fail. I question God, 'Why didn't I win? What happened?' But I need to remember that God was there. It was his plan.

"God has mapped out a lot of things in my life. I feel like there is a course he wants me to be on. But it's not a one-way relationship with God. It's something I have to put time into and it's something I have to work at, if I want to stay on the course that God has planned out. I have to remember that what he has planned is the right thing for me, no matter what I think. His plan is always better, his plan is always right."

He learned this lesson the hard way. He left high school a football hero, but his first year at Oklahoma University he sat on the bench. He was redshirted. He knew that he might be redshirted that first year. He tried to prepare himself. But nothing he did or thought was enough to prepare him for what lay ahead.

"In my head, I knew I wasn't quite ready for college ball," he admitted. "I knew that I needed time on the bench. But once we got a few games into the season and I wasn't playing, it was hard. I always started in high school. Whether it was football, basketball, or baseball, I always played. It was hard to sit on the bench. I didn't understand. I was miserable the whole time, not playing, sitting on the sideline. I thought God was punishing me for something. I felt like God abandoned me."

Sam stopped going to church and quit Fellowship of Christian Athletes (FCA) meetings. God seemed distant and the relationship felt strained. He thought God was supposed to make everything smooth and easy. But God didn't do that.

"Looking back, God hadn't abandoned me. He was preparing me for what he had ahead. I think he wanted me to know that my relationship with him wasn't just about football and success. When I realized what he was trying to teach me and how I had treated him, I was ashamed. I knew I had messed up. I had turned my back on God because he didn't give me what I wanted."

He learned to view God differently. God wasn't the genie in a bottle who made life perfect. He was the creator of the universe who has his own plans and who wants a relationship with his people.

"I realized I had to put time into my relationship with God. I struggle with trying to manage football, speaking engagements, and everything else I'm trying to do. Sometimes I don't put in the time I need to grow in that relationship with God. That is something I am always working on. But that is all part of the process.

"Living for God requires sacrifice. I have to put in a lot of effort to live the lifestyle that he would be proud of in a world where there's not a lot of self-discipline. I feel like when I live the life he wants for me, when my life encourages other people to honor God, in a small way I am saying thanks to God for all the blessings that he's given me. That's what life is really all about. I want people to see God for who he really is, and if my life can in some way help people see that, then I am a success, and it doesn't matter if I never touch a football again."

Sam Bradford won the Heisman trophy, college football's highest honor, in 2008. Two years later he was selected as the first overall draft pick by the St. Louis Rams, who offered him a record-breaking $78 million six year contract. He proved to be worth the money by breaking Peyton Manning's record for most rookie completions at 354.

Watch the Film

Sam Bradford
Iamsecond.com/sambradford

To see other stories like this, please visit:

Colt McCoy
Iamsecond.com/coltmccoy

Landry Jones
Iamsecond.com/landryjones

Baron Batch
Iamsecond.com/baronbatch

Booze and Batteries

Norm Miller

"My goals were simple. I wanted plenty of money and a great family. Nothing too crazy; I wasn't trying to be the next Bill Gates. I just wanted to be comfortable. By the time I was thirty-five, I reached those goals. I was making more money than I ever thought I would and had a beautiful wife and great kids that loved me. But I wasn't happy."

Norm traveled the country selling and setting up distributorships for Interstate Batteries, the company he would one day run. Every other week he hit the road and convinced shop owners to sell his batteries. The days were long and the work heavy. Drinking began as a way to relax after a long day's work. Then it became a way to go to sleep at night. It was a way to connect with coworkers, to have fun on the weekends. There was always a reason. Drinking seeped into every aspect of his life.

"For a long time I really did have fun. But then it got habitual. I couldn't stop. I started drinking as a way to deal with the pressure of business, as a way to deal with the long hours. After work, before bed, out with friends, my whole routine revolved around drinking. The more I drank the more I began relying on it, needing it to function."

The frost melted at the base of his mug. His arms rested

on the stained bar top. Tobacco burnt the air climbing through his throat. The cold ale brushed his tongue and warmed his gut. He didn't call his wife; he didn't want the argument. She would have dinner cooked and ready, but it would sit uneaten tonight.

Two DWIs marked his record, but tonight would be different. Only one drink, maybe two. But then it was three . . . four . . . five. He lost count. The booze glazed his eyes, calmed his mind, and ruined his resolve. The hours ticked by unnoticed until the taps closed and the bar emptied into the street. His keys clinked in his shaking hands. His steps wobbled toward the car. One miss, then two, then three, and the key finally slid into the hole. He cranked the engine and began his blurred drive home.

The lights burned his vision. The painted lines swayed across the road. In and out, faster and then slower, his mind clouded with the alcohol coursing in his veins. Flashing lights screamed behind him and pulled him to the shoulder.

"I had two DWIs and then I got stopped again," Norm recalled. "The officer, by God's grace, didn't check my record to see if I had any other convictions. He didn't even give me a ticket! I managed to make it back home. When I woke up the next morning, I remembered the night-time binge and the close call for yet a third DWI. The reality of my problem hit me then. I suddenly realized that I was out of control and my life was in peril. It wasn't a prayer. It wasn't a thought. It was like I hit my thumb with a hammer. In panic and desperation, I just blurted out in a half scream, 'God help me! I can't handle it!'

"If you had asked me a day before, I would have told you I didn't even know if I believed in God, I hadn't even thought about it. But something changed."

"Norm, you need to read the Bible," a friend challenged him days later.

Norm was a successful, hardworking career man with a promising future in the company, but something about life seemed empty. He needed alcohol to cool the pressure, the growing uneasiness in his soul. Every few days a pressure built inside—the emptiness, the unrest, the anxiety. It built to a tempest, forcing a release. Alcohol had soothed the angst for so long, so many years, but now it was too much. The blackout drunkenness, the DWIs, and the early morning bars continued, but the anxiety no longer eased.

"Why would I read the Bible?" Norm questioned. He had doubts.

"As far as I was concerned, the Bible was an old book written by a bunch of old guys that hadn't got anything to do with me."

But this friend continued to talk. He gave Norm some books to read and challenged him to search out the facts for himself. Norm began to read about the Bible. He studied all the arguments, the ancient histories and archeology. He examined the prophecies and their fulfillment, and the historical manuscript evidence for the Bible.

"If I was going to really base my whole life on something like the Bible, I wanted to know for sure if it was reliable. And the more I read and the more I studied, the more the facts forced me to believe that there had to be some truth in this book. So I started to read the Bible to see what it had to say about me.

"I wasn't thinking about eternal life or super spirituality. I was thinking about life here and now. My life was in shambles. I was unfulfilled and empty. I had thought that if I reached my goals I would be happy, but the reverse happened. I had all the money and success I ever wanted, but I was miserable and anxious. I wanted to know the truth. So I started reading the Bible to see if a person with a brain, with an intellect, could actually embrace it as truth."

He began reading the Bible, searching for truth, searching for meaning. Did the Bible make sense? Would it ring true? He entered a skeptic and left a believer.

"I came across a passage in Galatians chapter five that said the fruit of the Spirit is love, peace, and joy. I remember looking at that and thinking, *That's what I want. Circumstances don't make any difference. I can be white, black, short, tall, rich or poor; but if I've got love, peace, and joy, I've got life.*"

His wife went to church often and always asked him to come with her. He rarely agreed, but this Sunday he did. The class was taught by a middle-aged woman, smoking a cigarette as she paged through some book. The takeaway Norm got from her lesson was that God loved him, a simple message but one that connected with him.

"It struck me," he said. "God loved me? How could he love me? The things that I had done, the way I lived my life. I lived totally for myself. I was selfish and broken. I just assumed God didn't love me because of the way I lived. I never had a problem with the Bible telling me I was a sinner. I knew I was a sinner. I didn't even do what I wanted me to do, much less what God would want me to do. So hearing that God loved me, regardless of all the mess in my life, really hit me hard."

Norm was invited to another Bible study at a friend's house across town. The man leading it knew that Norm was still searching, still weighing his spiritual options. He asked questions and they talked until midnight. Norm was ready.

"I finally made the decision," Norm said. "I told God that I would make him first in my life. So I had to figure out what he wanted me to do. I got a Bible and started going to church. I decided that if the Bible was from God then I had to try and understand it."

His life had always been about money. How much could he make? How fast could he make it? Success was measured in dollars. Selling batteries was the only thing he cared about. But now that was changing.

"I realized that God did not measure success in dollars, but by love. He wanted me to love my neighbor. My barometer for success began to change. I started to measure how much I was experiencing God's love and how faithful I was in showing that love to others.

"At Interstate Batteries we took care of our distributors. John Searcy, the founder of the company, believed in this basic principle, that in business we should always treat people the way we would want to be treated. 'Do unto others' kind of thing. Go the extra mile for them. So that is what we did."

Norm was sent to Pasadena, where the local distributor had unexpectedly died. His wife panicked and shut down the business. She grounded the delivery trucks and closed the warehouse. The woman's newly acquired business would go bankrupt if left in this condition, and Interstate's reputation for timely delivery and service would be tainted. Norm was sent to remedy the problem.

Together, he and John Searcy convinced the widow that shuttering the business would leave her with nothing to sell. They arranged for an employee to take over the operations of the business. Interstate Batteries would fund the daily operations until a buyer could be found. And when it sold, she would receive the money in full.

"God brought a purpose to my life," Norm said. "He taught me what was really important. Life is more than money. Love is what matters. Helping people discover the truth of God and the Bible. These were the things that I became passionate about. I took over Interstate Batteries as chairman in 1978, and I had to figure out how to integrate this passion with running a company.

"I wrestled with knowing how bold I should be in business about my faith. I could lose employees. I could lose business or face lawsuits. Then I came across a verse in Matthew 10:28 that basically said, 'Don't fear, but if you do, fear him who can do something to you after you're dead!' So I prayed for boldness to share Jesus with the people in my business. I prayed for wisdom, for the words to say, and that I wouldn't offend anyone.

"I never give preference to Christians in my business. Everyone is treated equally. I respect everyone's beliefs and personal decisions, but I am not shy about my faith. I strive to be both sensitive and bold in sharing the love and message of Jesus in my life and in my business. I want to be known not just as the guy who sold batteries but also as a man who shared God's love."

Norm Miller began as a traveling salesman for Interstate Batteries and today is the face and Chairman of the company. And it was his vision and passion for sharing God's love that gave birth to the I am Second movement.

To see other stories like this, please visit:

Joe Gibbs
Iamsecond.com/joegibbs

Wayne Huizenga
Iamsecond.com/waynehuizenga

Darrell Waltrip
Iamsecond.com/darrellwaltrip

Hooker for Jesus

Annie Lobert

Annie Lobert dreamed of Prince Charming, of Prince Rescue-the-Girl, and Prince Whisk-Me-Away. Dad played the villain in her fairytale. Distant and cold. Loud and angry. Other little girls had dads that loved them, spoke sweet words, hugged and kissed them. But not her. Maybe he loved her. What father didn't? But his love hid behind a wall of rage and a dark closet of his own childhood abuse. He never knew the look of love, the soft touch of kindness, the warm words and quiet hugs. He only knew coldness and he gave plenty of coldness in return. He wielded his strength with anger, his manliness with malice. Fatherly care and protection yielded to emotional brutality, fury, and alcohol.

Within Annie grew a heart with a daddy-sized hole. She hoped for a prince that could fill this void, a rescuer, a lover, a father-like caretaker who would fill the longing of a daddy-less childhood. She dreamed of hearing those three little words that bring magic and life to the heart of every girl. She dreamed of one day hearing from a man, "I love you."

"I used to dream I was a princess," she recalled, "that I had wicked stepparents and one day a prince on a beautiful white horse would come rescue me and take me away from the evil castle. I never heard my dad say that he loved me. I just remember my dad raging; coming home and acting in a way that I didn't understand. I thought I must be unlovable. I needed to know that I was loved, but I never heard the words from my dad, so I dreamed of Prince Charming."

As high school dawned, she found boys paying attention to her.

"I gravitated toward any compliment, any pass that was made at me," she remembered. "Any boy who wrote a note, 'Do you like me? Circle yes or no.' I started to feel alive inside in a way that I had never felt before."

"I met a boy who completely stole my heart," she said. "He told me if I slept with him we'd get married. He gave me his ring. He told me he loved me, that we would start a life together, have babies. I felt like my fantasies were coming true, that I could really be loved."

She reckoned him her prince and gave her all to him; body, love, and affections. "I took my entire heart and gave it to this boy," she confessed. "I gave up my virginity to him. I gave him everything."

But he betrayed her gift. She caught this boy in knight's apparel visiting the beds of other girls. This never happened in the fairytales, never in the romantic comedies or cable TV broadcasts. Love proved a much more evasive creature in real life.

"This can't be true!" she thought. "This cannot be happening!"

Everything she knew of love came from television and romance novels and this never happened in those stories. This betrayal soured into self-doubt, anger, and rebellion.

The words "I must be unlovable" rolled around her head all the more loudly.

"I became convinced that there must be something wrong with me," she said. "I felt no love from my dad, betrayed by this boy. I searched for love and came up empty. I didn't even love myself."

Before her cap and gown even had a chance to wrinkle, Annie left her small town and went out on her own. Escaping the anger of home and the pain of her high school betrayal, she landed in Minneapolis. She vowed never to return to those tormented memories. She ventured to see if the world could really deliver all it promised.

"My heart was broken," she said, "and I decided to rebel. I took culture's pill. I wanted to try and see if it really was as glamorous as it seemed in the movies and magazines."

The nightclubs became her medicine. She could walk into a club and find men happy to oblige her craving for love and attention. Clubs were her haven, the place she went to find desperate love, even the temporary kind. However, what began as occasional turned obsessive. The alcohol that took the soul of her father began to take hers. The drugs, the sex, and the rebellion began to possess her instead of the other way around.

"I would drink and black out," Annie confessed. "I would smoke pot and black out. I would still go to work. I'd never be late. Never miss a day of work. Didn't matter how hungover I was, but I was a party girl. Money made it possible. If I made money, if I had nice clothes, if I went out to the clubs, I could meet different men that liked me. Maybe I could meet a rich guy that would sweep me off my feet and take care of me."

One winter night, Annie and a girlfriend slipped on their dresses, walked into a club, and found a seat at the bar. Like bait on a hook, they sat waiting, hoping, and dreaming.

Maybe just maybe, they thought, someone rich, someone able to care for them, to love them, would notice them that night. They sipped dry their drinks, smiled, and chatted, praying for their prey to bite.

Two men approached the bar where they sat. Donned with fur coats and Rolex watches, the men bought Annie and her friend drinks. They boasted of wealth, real estate, and businesses. The drinks were a compliment but their money a coveted temptation. Months later, when her friend got engaged to one of them, with a twenty-thousand dollar ring, Annie lusted for the money.

"I was tired of working three jobs," Annie said. "I was enticed by the lifestyle that money could buy. I told my girl-friend to get that guy's money. I had built this vendetta inside of me, this deep rooted unforgiveness toward my dad, toward that boy in school. I wanted revenge. Money was going to be the answer."

Her friend ran off to Hawaii with her new fiancé and called Annie to join her.

"I am on the beach in a drop top Corvette," her friend bragged. "You need to come out here. I know how we can make some real money."

"I couldn't say no," Annie said. "I knew it didn't seem right, that something seemed off, but I didn't have the guts to ask her. I just went with it. It was the lure of nice things, of finally having money. I flew to Hawaii, met up with my girlfriend, and that first night on the beach we sold ourselves to some Japanese clients. And I became a prostitute.

"I went back to Minnesota with a completely skewed perspective on life. Once I found out that I could make hun-dreds of dollars, thousands even, by selling myself with no attachment, no relationship, it gave me this immense power. No longer could $3.47 an hour cut it. Now it was $500 an hour, $1,000 an hour, $2,000, and if you wanted me for the night, that was $10,000."

She started moonlighting at escort services in Minneapolis. Men would find her ad, a picture, a number, and she'd come directly to their room. She soon quit all three of her jobs and started exotic dancing as well.

"A few months later, I met Travis," she said. "He walked in and spread a fan of hundred dollar bills at my feet. I danced for him. He had this charisma, this charm, a debonair way about him. I cannot describe it, he just drew me in and we started dating."

He gave her roses and presents, dinners, and jewelry. He said all the right things.

"You're beautiful," he would say. "You are so intelligent."

"Wow! This man is telling me I'm beautiful," she said. "He's telling me I'm smart and pretty, that he loves me. My heart was just overwhelmed with joy. Here was my dream coming true. He dressed me nice, complimented me. He was everything my dad never was. He saw the hole in my heart and knew exactly how to fill it. I thought he would be the one to rescue me."

She wanted to move to Las Vegas and convinced Travis to join her. The opportunities, the money, the neon lights, even her best friend from Hawaii was now in Vegas, and it all beckoned her lust and imagination.

"The first night we flew into Las Vegas, I got off the plane and walked the strip. I signed up for an escort service, made two calls, and came home with a wad of cash."

This would be their new life, she thought, rich clients

and easy money. She glowed with excitement about the future she and Travis could soon buy. She returned home, tossed her purse on the table, and slipped off her heals. The lights from the strip still glowed in her eyes. The new hope of a new city still gleamed on her face. With her shoes hanging from her fingers, Annie straightened her back and paused, seeing Travis brooding quietly across the room. He suddenly looked dark and dangerous. The warmth had drained from his face and something strange and unexpected filled its place; a quiet rage she had seen before, an anger and unsettlingly evil. She knew this look in other men, but never Travis.

"Break yourself," Travis suddenly demanded, pimp language for "give me all your money."

"What?" Annie responded with disbelief gasping in her voice. Her face tingled with shock. Tears forced their way into her eyes.

"You heard me," he responded. "Break yourself. Dump your purse out on my lap."

"What are you talking . . ." But before she finished, he leaped from his chair and slammed his palm into her throat, his fingers gripping around her neck.

"Giv't to me!" he screamed, rage slurring his voice. He swung his body forward slinging her into the kitchen. He threw his leg into her side and kicked into her back as she squirmed on the floor. He grabbed her hair and dragged her back through the house. She screamed and pleaded, begging for release.

"I am your pimp now," he shouted as she clawed his arms in a desperate attempt to escape. Her skin burned as it skidded across the carpet, blood spilling from her wounds. With a violent jerk, he flung her through the back door onto the porch. Clumps of blood and hair clung to his still clenched fists. Her nose twisted and her ribs snapped as his unfettered fury flowed into her broken body.

"Stop! Please, stop!" she cried to the man turned monster, but the blows continued until she lay swollen and bloodied in the grass and mud of the backyard.

"I'm your pimp," he said with ice in his lungs. "You're going to work for me. You will pay me whether you like it or not. And if you try to leave, I'll kill you."

"I looked in his eyes," she recalled, "and it was like looking at the devil. I couldn't believe somebody could hate me so much. All this because I didn't hand over my money to him. This man who professed his love to me, this man whom I trusted, believed in, committed to spend my life with was beating me telling me that he hated me. But there was something inside me that still loved him."

Later that night, as she lay in bed crying, he came in and lay down next to her. He wrapped his arms around her.

"Don't cry," he said. "Shhhh. Don't cry. I love you. Don't you know, you made me do this? You have to submit to me if you want this to work. I do this to protect you."

"That night, I died inside," Annie said. "I knew that if I tried to escape, he'd hunt me down. The next five years of my life I was with a pimp. Today, they call it sex trafficking, but I didn't think of it like that, because I loved him. Every time he hit me, choked me, raped me, made me train young girls, or put guns to my head, I did it because I loved and feared him."

"I was with a monster, the prince that turned dark. But there was something inside of me that thought I could change him. I thought I could fix him with my love. The more that I obeyed him, the more I thought he would love me. I saw this hurt little boy, abused by his mother, who didn't know any better. He had been on the street since he was young. I felt compelled to fix him with my love."

He took her to a house with other prostitutes that was run by him and his friends. He shaved her head, stripped her naked, and beat her for hours. He spit on her and threatened death if she ever left, ever failed to give up her money, jewelry, cars, everything.

"I had long, golden blonde hair and he took it from me," she said. "He broke me. He convinced me that I deserved this treatment, that I earned all this pain and abuse. It was years before I ever dared leave and when I did, I had nothing, because when you leave a pimp, you leave with nothing. "

She escaped her pimp but not the sex industry. She found work with another escort service. She made her calls and earned her money, but not like before. It wasn't the same. But at least it was all hers now. No giving it up to a pimp. Then she got cancer and life took another turn for the worse. She went on chemotherapy, and, for the second time, she lost her hair.

"I remember laying there in my bed looking in the mirror, thinking that God must be so angry with me, that this must be punishment for my lifestyle. I went on calls wearing wigs, because my hair was gone. Clients starting asking for their money back saying I lied to them, that I was sick, and that they weren't going to pay. I'd go home and just cry. I would get in the shower, scrub my body and think I'll never, ever be clean. "

She started taking pain medicines. First, it was for the pain related to her cancer, but then she used it to numb all the other pain in her life. That led to other drugs and those led to cocaine. Her house and possessions were sold to pay for her habit.

"I went down this dark road," she said. "I was living in my car or in seedy motels. Then one night, I decided to get higher than I ever had before. I just wanted to erase all of the pain, the pain of the past, the cancer, the abuse. I had lost so many years living in Las Vegas away from my family. I lost everything I had ever earned whether through Travis or now my drug problems. I took a big hit of coke and I fell back."

The floor thumped as her head struck the carpet but she felt no pain. The overhead light went dim and then completely dark. She fell paralyzed and blind. Her heart raced in her throat and then abruptly stopped.

"I felt this demonic presence come over me. I was raised in church, but I didn't know God. I thought he hated me. But that night I got scared. I knew I was at death's door. I was in this dark, dark cave. I saw my family. I saw my funeral. I was in the coffin. Everybody was crying, wiping their faces. They were saying, 'She was just a prostitute.' And that's when I said, 'Jesus. Please save me. I don't know if you're real, but I don't want to die.' Then I woke up and I was in the hospital."

"You are lucky to be alive," a doctor said, holding her hand. "You have so much drugs in your system, little lady, you should be dead. God must be with you."

"And I knew that Jesus had heard my prayer," she said. "I had this peace come over me that was nothing like I'd ever felt in my entire life. No amount of money, no amount of sex, no amount of drugs could ever replicate that feeling. No amount of cars or jewelry could make me feel the way I felt in that hospital bed. I could feel the Holy Spirit just fill me with liquid love and I knew I was forgiven. I knew it. I knew God gave me a second chance. I knew he had finally made me clean. I knew that he loved me. My prince had finally come and his name was Jesus."

She slowly began piecing her life back together. She got clean of the drugs, left the sex industry, started reading her Bible and even began meeting with others who also followed Jesus. That terrified her the most.

"Won't they judge me?" she thought. "Won't they hate me and criticize me? I'm an ex-prostitute, after all."

But all she found was love, forgiveness, and open arms.

Forgiveness seemed the hardest lesson to learn in her own life. Learning to forgive her dad, that boy in high school, all the men, friends, and people that had hurt and abused her was a long and gradual process. However, forgiving herself proved the biggest hurdle.

"I learned to forgive those who'd hurt me," she said. "It was a process. The hardest challenge was forgiving myself. I still struggle with that. I think that is a stronghold for a lot of people, but I also had to ask for a lot of forgiveness. I hurt a lot of people. My drug addiction took me to a lot of dark places, but in the end relationships have been healed. Even my dad and I have reconciled."

It was Christmas Eve and Annie was at home with her father. She had finally told her family about the life she had lived and the lies she had told. He sat at the kitchen table while she made him some juice.

"Dad, I'm making this juice for you," she said. "I am making it for you because I love you."

The man who never cried, began to cry.

"I'm so sorry," he said. "I am so sorry for the way I treated you kids growing up. I never wanted to hurt you."

"I hugged him," she recalled. "Something happened between me and my dad that day. I had planned to confront him about the pain he had caused and to tell him that I had forgiven him, but I never had to. He knew. He told me he loved me that he was proud of how far I had come. It took me years to feel comfortable enough to talk with him about it all. Sometimes people want everything to work out quick, but I prayed for a couple years and it was well worth the wait."

Just when life began to feel normal, she heard a new calling. She heard a voice. Audible or not, she could never tell, but she heard it as clear as rain on a tin roof.

"Annie, I want you to go back down to that strip," the voice said. "I want you to tell the girls in slavery that I love them."

"I hesitated," she admitted. "I can die doing that. I've got pimps that don't like me. Death threats from old clients and an old life."

God argued back, "If you can walk down a dark hallway and knock on a door of a trick, a John, a client that you don't know, not knowing what is on the other side, then you can do this for me."

"I can," she confessed, "because I know that you are with me."

With that Hookers for Jesus was founded. Annie started walking down the same strip, the same streets, and back alleyways and dark corners of the city that she used to call home, telling all who would listen that Jesus loved them. Whether hooker or pimp, she told them all about Jesus.

"I don't hate pimps," she said. "I don't cuss them out or yell at them, and I have every reason to hate. But I don't.

When I see a pimp, I talk to them, tell them about Jesus, what he has done in my life, and what he can do in theirs."

"And when I see a girl that is in the same place that I was, she's my sister. I feel I have to just reach out to her, take her hand, and let her know that she's going to be okay. I feel this protective, strong compassion, the compulsion to just tell them, 'You can get up now. God has forgiven you.'

"Yes, I was a hooker. Yes, I was a prostitute, but no longer. I was redeemed, made new and clean. No longer did I hook people for sex and money, I hooked them for Jesus. 'I will make you fishers of men,' Jesus said. And that is exactly what I set out to do."

She spoke a simple message. The message she spent her life never hearing but always missing, a message of love. She went around speaking those three little words every girl needs to hear, but so few do.

"Just tell the girls that I love them," she heard Jesus saying. "Tell them they're forgiven. Tell them that I hung around girls just like them. Tell them to read my gospels."

"No matter where you've been, no matter what you've done, no matter how dirty you feel, there's redemption. You are white as snow when you accept Jesus into your heart. Women are getting set free, and it's so simple. It's not about a program. It's not about giving a girl a food card, or a clothing card, or providing a place for her to stay, or providing a hotel for her, or even just bringing her to church. It's about holding her in your arms, hugging her, loving her, looking into her eyes, and telling her that she's loved by the Founder of the universe, by her almighty Creator, her Daddy, her real Daddy. Las Vegas has become grace city. It's the city of lights to us, because us women who walk on the strip at night, we shine for him."

"Little girl lost," she said, recalling her story. "Thought no one loved her. Thought no one wanted her. Ran away from her castle. She was embraced by the Devil and his false love. And through that embracing became a different person. Became the harlot. Became the queen of lies. The Jezebel. But God met her on that dark road. And when she was at her lowest point, when everyone else had left her, and forsaken her, he pulled her out of that well, that dark empty well. He took her in his arms, and he walked her home, back to the castle where she was born. He gave her the golden scepter, and said, 'Daughter, go rescue my daughters.'"

Annie Lobert continues to walk the streets of Las Vegas telling girls and pimps alike that Jesus loves them. Her organization, Hookers for Jesus, reaches out to the most desperate of our world telling them that God forgives them. Through a partnership with her local church Destiny House was also founded, a beautiful half-way home designed to provide transitional housing for the women that Hookers of Jesus rescues from sex trafficking.

Watch the Film

Annie Lobert
Iamsecond.com/annielobert

To see other stories like this, please visit:

Karen Green
Iamsecond.com/karengreen

The Business of Beauty

Kathy Ireland

"Dlo? Dlo?" the boy asked in Creole, hoping for water. Dust and blood still crusted the wandering faces of his city. Buried souls still cried from the rubble but most would soon wane and grow quiet. More than 200,000 would die. Thousands more would later succumb to dysentery and cholera. The temporary tent relief areas would turn to permanent dwellings of squalor as governments and aid organizations struggled to rebuild.

But this boy only thought of water. The worries of disease and starvation, ruined homes and infrastructure dimmed with the onset of parched lips and a dry throat. Behind him stood a crowd of children, all equally parched, each echoing the boy's request for water. Their eyes pierced through the dusty air and bore into the heart of Kathy Ireland as she stood there wishing she could do more to help.

"Dlo? Dlo?" the boy and the other children continued to beg with outstretched hands.

Their gaunt faces and glassy eyes told of death stalking, but Kathy had no water. She had given her last bottle of water to other empty hands and dry throats. All her gifts, all her prayers, all her water, and all her food seemed a speck of sand along the beach. What could be done in the face of such disaster? What could be done with so many thirsty faces?

Kathy had joined the relief efforts in Haiti shortly after the earthquake struck that leveled much of the country. She was stationed at a camp near a ravine that held seventeen hundred survivors. They each huddled on sheets spread across the ground or shaped into makeshift tents. After a few violent shakes from the earth, all of them were now homeless.

"God, please multiply the water," Kathy whispered in anguish, as she looked into the boy's face. She thought of the miracles she had read of Jesus healing the maimed, feeding the hungry, giving drink to the thirsty. She thought of Jesus feeding the five thousand with a few loaves of bread and some fish. She dreamed of the thousands being fed once again, of thousands having their thirst quenched and their wounds healed, but no such miracle arrived. Death had already taken so many, and so many more would soon feel its cold grasp. And to those who survived, thirst, hunger, and suffering would become a daily burden.

The children's small, thirsty voices still tugged at her heart as she stood with empty hands. She had nothing to offer and nothing to sway the wave of despair rushing across their faces. Just then, a fellow relief worker stepped out from under a medical tent, and hearing the children's cries, motioned them over. Together, he and Kathy grabbed a stack of small paper cups and began passing them into the small dirty hands that stood before them. The band of children surged forward as the hope of water became a reality. Three bottles of water rested on the table and soon each tiny cup was filled with an equally tiny portion of water, hardly a swallow. Smiles and laugher could be heard as the cups filled. Delight shone on their faces for this small gift, a necessity of life so often taken for granted but now held so precious.

This world of hunger and thirst, devastation and ruin, was not a world that Kathy had ever known. She lived the storied life of a supermodel turned billion dollar business mogul. She first graced the stage of modeling while still in high school and, upon graduation, landed in Paris to continue what would become one of the most successful modeling careers of her generation.

"While it might sound glamorous, that first stay in Paris was a lonely one," she confessed, thinking back to those early days of modeling. She lived in a home with other models. Her room stood at the end of a long, dark hallway. The room's previous residents called it "the dungeon." Many slow, lonely hours withered away in that room. It was before internet, before cell phones. There was no television. Silence and boredom were the only luxuries.

On one particular night, as midnight slipped into morning, when loneliness fell into an agonizing storm of restlessness, she searched through her bag and found an unexpected gift; a Bible unknowingly stuffed in her bag.

"Mom," she said aloud with a slight smile, her hands grasping the book.

They all used to go church when Kathy was younger, but it was out of guilt and habit rather than conviction. With time, the habit faded and church became a memory. They didn't disbelieve in God or dislike the thought of Jesus. It was just that it all seemed distant, somehow intangible.

Years later, her mom met a friend who made her rethink everything. The woman had a peace about her. It wasn't that the woman's life was easy or even all that unusual. Her life still had its struggles, still had its ups and downs, but somehow this friend had a peace through it all. Something or someone seemed to guide her and comfort her through all her storms. Even despite the pressures and stresses of raising teenage daughters, the woman was at ease with life. She discovered that the woman's peace wasn't a religion and it wasn't a self-help fad, it was Jesus. Wanting that peace for herself, she began to follow Jesus anew.

"Mom was really quiet about her faith in the beginning," Kathy said. "But I was noticing this transformation in her. I liked what I saw. When I saw that Bible in my bag, I knew she had put it there."

With nothing else to do and sleep still far from her eyes, Kathy opened the leather bound pages. Her fingers flipped through the pages and found one that recounted the life, teaching, death, and resurrection of Jesus. She read the story of Matthew; a wealthy tax collector who stumbled upon a man named Jesus, and was never the same again.

Kathy had heard sermons and remembered her church days, but never had she read the Bible herself, never had she read the stories of Jesus with her own eyes.

"If you had asked me if I was a Christian before that night, I would have said yes. I believed in God. I never remember a time when I didn't believe in God. But something was missing. It was more a religion than a personal relationship with God. I viewed God as this angry, condemning God, instead of a loving personal God who cared about me."

But, as one page passed over another, and another, and the night grew deep, she met a new kind of Jesus. Those pages revealed a loving God, a loving Jesus. It wasn't the stiff, angry Jesus she had remembered from church as a child.

"Jesus wasn't anything like I thought," she recalled. "He wasn't condemning. He wasn't yelling. He was loving. I remember reading the story of the Samaritan woman. His followers couldn't understand why Jesus would talk to a Samaritan, since Jews and Samaritans didn't get along. But even more so, they couldn't believe he would talk to a Samaritan woman, and a highly immoral, disreputable woman on top of that. He was honest with her. He didn't ignore her immoralities, but he addressed her with such love and such respect. It completely surprised me."

"While I had always believed in God, I certainly didn't know him. This was a God, this was a Jesus I knew nothing about. I discovered him for the first time reading through those pages. I finally began to understand why mom seemed so different, why her faith became so real to her. It was no longer just about faith or religion, it was about knowing a God that truly and genuinely loved me as an individual."

Despite her new found relationship with God, questions remained. Questions, particularly about the Bible, still haunted her. Old patterns died slowly.

"There were verses I would come across that I thought must surely be a typo," she admitted. "I started to pick and choose the parts of the Bible I liked or didn't like. I tried to fit God in this box, this mold of what I wanted. I found passages that I liked and I would read them over and over again. If I read something I didn't like or didn't understand, I found some way to explain it away. But this habit stunted my growth and my relationship with God for years. I became stuck at this young immature spiritual place."

"But God was so patient with me, despite my failures," she confessed. "The hardest thing was giving up control to God, really trusting him in everything. But that relationship with God gave me the strength to walk away from a lot of compromising situations. He guided me as I progressed in my modeling career.

"Modeling was never part of my plan," she said. "I was trying and failing at all these different businesses trying to find something else. If I would have been successful at one of those businesses early on, I wouldn't have gone on so long in that industry."

But despite her many business flops, success seemed ever-present in her modeling career. She found herself on the cover of *Sports Illustrated's* legendary swimsuit edition three times, the first of which became *SI's* best-selling edition ever. She went on to grace its pages consecutively for more than a decade. She made her big screen debut with a starring role in *Alien in L.A.* and appeared again in a 1989 reinterpretation of Jules Verne's *Journey to the Center of the Earth*, as well as dozens of television movies and sitcom cameos. Her fame and success spread even further with the release of numerous workout videos. She, along with the likes of Christie Brinkley and Cindy Crawford, spawned a whole new genre of model, the supermodel.

But, despite her modeling stardom, she is perhaps best known for her line of licensed clothes, jewelry, household products, and even bridal dresses and destinations that all began with a simple pair of socks. Socks were an odd venture for a high-glam, world-renowned beauty, but socks made her brand and her name connect with the everyday woman. In 1994, her surprise sock venture helped land her a long-term licensing agreement with a major retailer. This opportunity eventually allowed for products designed by Kathy, from workout clothes to dresses and shoes, to be distributed and sold throughout the country.

"I loved business and design," she said. "I didn't know exactly what I wanted to do, but I liked the idea of building something. Even as a kid, I was obsessed with business. My first enterprise was selling painted rocks out of a little wagon in my neighborhood. "

From there, she ventured beyond the familiar world of fashion and clothes and moved into furniture. Her original venture in socks endeared her to the everyday woman and furniture would be no different. ". . . Finding solutions for families, especially busy moms" became the mantra and later official slogan of her fledgling empire. It wasn't about the money. If it didn't help busy moms and families, her name wouldn't be found on the package. She insisted everything have a purpose. It came from a core desire to help women like her—busy moms who still wanted to care for their families.

Despite her unorthodox venture in socks and furniture, or perhaps because of it, Kathy Ireland built one of the most successful licensing companies in the world. Today, Forbes magazine estimates that the 15,000 products that bear her name equal more than $2 billion in retail sales. This staggering sum more than doubles the $900 million worth of sales that Martha Stewart is estimated to bring in.

Despite all her success, her beauty, her wildly lucrative business, nothing replaced the relationship that started so many years ago in the dungeon.

"I went to church as a kid, but I never read the Bible," she said. "When I finally opened it up, years later, in that lonely room, I feel like I met Jesus for the first time. I was alone. No one was talking to me, influencing me. It was just me and the Bible. I didn't read and think I wanted to be this religion, or that religion. I just read it. What I discovered was a God who loved me. I found Jesus, a man who treated women with so much love and respect and in a culture that mistreated women so badly. It was a Jesus I never knew existed."

"I decided then, that I was going to follow Jesus. God loved me, and I fell in love with him. And despite all the messes I've made, he keeps cleaning all of them up. He wants to be front and center in my life. It hasn't been easy, especially for someone so independently minded like me. But letting Him be first, it is so freeing.

"When I first started modeling and I started to follow Jesus, I read that Jesus said it was more difficult for a camel to go through the eye of a needle than for a rich man to enter the kingdom of God. I've had to learn that money is just a thing, and that loving money ruins everything. Money can't buy happiness and it doesn't give peace. Only God can do that.

"People ask me what my goals are. It's simple. My goal is to grow closer to Jesus each day, to follow his lead and stay on his path. I'm a work in progress. I get distracted. I put my career or busy schedule ahead of God. I put my family first, but whether it's through the thirsty voices of those children in Haiti, or during those quite moments in prayer, God always reminds me that he is the only one who deserves to be first."

While Kathy Ireland no longer models for *Sports Illustrated*, *Cosmopolitan*, or *Vogue*, she continues to inspire a brand of beauty that goes beyond bathing suits, a beauty of the soul. Her licensing company, kathy ireland Worldwide, continues to grow and help busy families and busy moms. But, as always, it all takes second place to the God she met that lonely night in Paris.

Watch the Film

Kathy Ireland
Iamsecond.com/kathyireland

To see other stories like this, please visit:

Myrka Dellanos
Iamsecond.com/myrkadellanos

Lauren Scruggs
Iamsecond.com/laurenscruggs

Owning
Success

Darrell Waltrip

Darrell Waltrip first drove onto the NASCAR scene
in a 1971 Mercury Cyclone with a rented crew chief, a handful
of spare parts, and a head full of dreams. It was Talladega,
Alabama at the Alabama International Motor Speedway. The
track was completed barely two years prior and raised more
than one eyebrow with its unusually high 30 degree banks
and consequent blistering speeds. But undeterred rookie
Waltrip donned his Goodyear uniform and qualified 25th
only to exit the race with a blown engine after 69 of 188 laps.

His career began without fanfare and his first race ended
with a mere 680 dollar payout. But his status as a racing leg-
end began to take shape just a few years later, when in 1975,
he finished seventh in NASCAR's top racing series. He would
go on to fifteen straight years of top ten series rankings
including three championship wins.

"I was in my prime," Waltrip recalls, "We were unbeat-
able. We'd roll into town and just ask, 'Where's the winner's
circle?' Because we knew that's where we would end up."

The '81 and '82 years were especially successful, with
a combined 24 race wins and two series championships.
Waltrip dominated the field.

"I loved when I would show up for a race, check into a

hotel and the lady behind the counter would ask if I was there for the show. I would smile and just say, 'No ma'am, I am the show.'

"It was a dream come true for me." Waltrip says, looking back on nearly three decades of driving in NASCAR. "I always wanted to race, but now I was winning too.

"There is something about sitting in that driver's seat, it's like riding a beast. It's not just the competition of racing the other guy, it's going down a straightaway into a corner at 200 plus miles per hour. fighting a car that wants to go one way while you want to go another. It's a thrill, a challenge. People say racing looks so easy, but that's the art, the beauty of racing. If you do it right, it does look easy. Only a driver knows how much effort and work it takes to do it well."

But racing consumed every aspect of his life. Living on the road, hotel to hotel, one track to another.

"I put my wife through hell a number of times through those years," he admits. "My mistress was racing."

The Waltrips wanted to have children and to start a family, but Darrell never made the time. His racing took front stage. He didn't have time for a family and barely had time for his marriage.

"I promised her the world, a life of excitement," he recalls. "She would come to my races sit on a toolbox in the pits at Talladega or Martinsville or wherever I happened to be. She could see the races like no one else, but she didn't have a clue the kind of life I was really promising when we first married. She didn't know my heart was really on the track, not in our marriage. Our marriage hit some real tough times during those years. I was so consumed by my racing career that if she had left me, I probably wouldn't have even really cared at the time."

"I think it was the selfishness and the arrogance," he admits. "Nobody really wanted to be around me. They stuck around because I was a winning NASCAR driver, not because I was a nice guy."

Success and fame and money poured in with every new race and every new victory, but it all began to eat away at his personality, at who he was. Maybe it revealed the selfishness that always lay deep inside or maybe the selfishness sprouted from the constant attention and praise. But selfish is who he became. Everyone could see it but him.

"People call it cockiness, arrogance," Waltrip says, "all those adjectives that describe a successful athlete. But I didn't even realize what an arrogant jerk I had become. I was the guy who got all the accolades. I was the guy everyone wanted to have their picture with and get an autograph from. But it all started to change me. I told myself it was just confidence, but it was so much worse than that."

"And nothing was ever my fault," he recalls. "I was perfect. I didn't screw up the pit stop. I didn't build the engine that blew. I wasn't the idiot who ran into me. I just blamed everybody around me."

People still wanted to work with Waltrip but not because of his personality. He was a winner. Mistakes were beneath him and anyone who made one was beneath him as well. People got fired for simple errors, even if it wasn't their own. But somebody had to be blamed. For everyone that was let go, there were more that rushed in to join the team. But despite being surrounded by people clamoring to work with him, it was a lonely popularity. People hung around to work on a winning car not to be with an arrogant driver.

"It was a hard thing to come to grips with," he says. "There were actually people who worked with me that didn't like me. Matter of fact, they despised me because of my arrogance. They tolerated me because of what I did, but they still hated me.

"Even the fans started to hate me," he recalled in half disbelief. "They booed me, wore shirts that said 'Anbody but Waltrip,' they threw beer cans and chicken bones at me. I was winning, but they all hated me. Even Richard Petty said that I may win a lot of races and make a lot of money, but I will never be NASCAR's most popular driver, and he was right. That's what was so hard. I knew he was right. I knew they hated me."

But after two years of huge success in '81 and '82, his pride smashed into a wall at the opening race of the '83 season at Daytona. Waltrip pulled out of a turn on lap 62, trailing driver Richard Brooks, when Brooks hit the brakes. Waltrip, without time or space to react, hit Brooks, spun off the track, and slammed into the interior barrier wall. His car, crushed on one side, was thrown back across the track, slipped through 200 mile per hour traffic, and rear ended the outside wall. His number 11 car finally skidded to a rest at the bottom of the track with Waltrip unconscious, sitting inside.

"I came to on the way to the hospital," he recalled. "I had a serious concussion but that was in the days when we didn't really know how serious those things can be. They checked me over and sent me on home. I don't remember the next two weeks of my life."

The next week, his head still throbbing, he went on to race at Richmond where he qualified fourth. The week after that was Rockingham, North Carolina where he finished third. People noticed he was acting odd. But Waltrip was always a little odd, so they ignored it. But then he finally came out of the haze.

"I raced in Richmond and I had raced in Rockingham," he remembered. "But I couldn't remember either. It was frightening. I had done all these things. I was at the top of my game. But it was right at that moment, after having missed two weeks of my life, that I realized I could have died. I was mortal. I had never been so scared in my life."

He started to attend a Bible study that met in the cafeteria of a local school. His strained marriage, the crowds hating him, coworkers despising him, and now the realization that death was real, that his life could end any day on the track. It all started to crowd into his mind, made him ask the bigger questions. Soon the leader of his Bible study challenged him, asked him if he believed in Jesus Christ as his Lord and Savior.

"I think it was just everything in my life mushrooming in my mind," Waltrip said. "I'd had incredible success, but I now knew it could all be taken away. Suddenly, success wasn't all I thought it was. I thought I owned success, that it was all mine. I thought I was the one driving my life, but I didn't own success. Jesus owned it. I thought I was the star, but he is the real star. The difference between me and him is I wanted to keep all the success for myself, but Jesus just wanted to share with us."

"So in that moment I got on my knees, sweaty, no air conditioning, crying in the hallway, and asked Jesus to come into my life, to forgive me for my arrogance and all my mistakes. And I gotta' say, '83 turned out to be a great year. Not so great on the track, but personally, in my relationships, my marriage, everything started to turn in the right direction."

Darrell Waltrip continued to race for more than a decade. He won another national championship in 1985, was awarded most popular driver in 1989 and again in 1990. He went on to become the Fox Sports and SPEED commentator and in 2012, he was officially inducted into the NASCAR Hall of Fame.

Watch the Film

Darrell Waltrip
Iamsecond.com/darrellwaltrip

To see other stories like this, please visit:

Trevor Bayne
Iamsecond.com/trevorbayne

NASCAR Drivers
Iamsecond.com/NASCARdrivers

Significant
Beats

Lecrae

"Five forty six in the morning,
Tossing and turning.
Chest burning.
Sermons in my head keep reoccurring.
Having visions in my head
Of a kid crying at the feet of the Father
For all the wrong things that he did.
Now, I'm sweating in my sheets.
Can't sleep,
'Cause my mind keeps telling me I'm six feet deep.
Don't remind me.
Even though I'm still alive, I can't tell.
The way I'm living my life, I feel I'm going to hell."

—Lecrae

"My mother was a single parent," Lecrae said. **"My** dad lost himself in drugs and let his life crumble. I never knew him. Never met him or had a conversation with him. Not having a biological father makes a young man wrestle with significance and identity."

A latchkey kid, home alone, growing up on television,

and hip hop and urban culture, Lecrae just wanted to belong. The men he knew, his uncles, the guys in his neighborhood, became his role models. It never matters to a young boy whether the men surrounding them are good or bad, upright or evil, just that they are accepted by them. Young men gravitate to whoever bestows significance and value and acceptance.

"My uncles were leaders in the community," he said. "Whether it was gangs or drugs, they were known. They were leaders. They were cool guys in my mind. It didn't matter if they were doing terrible things or if they were good people or bad. I just wanted to fit in, and they gave me a sense of credibility. People embraced me and accepted me because of them."

No dad, poor role models, the general boredom of being home alone, and this intense desire to fit in, combined into a nasty stew of misbehavior: small theft, graffiti, troublemaking.

"I grabbed a BB gun one day, stood in the middle of the street, and pointed it at a car. The lady driving towards me freaked out. Started backing up and squealing her tires. I just thought it was fun, until the cops came and tackled me to the ground. I was always getting in trouble trying to fit in."

Hip hop music gave voice to his angst, this search for significance. He longed to find his place in the world, to find an idol to follow. There were no more Martin Luther Kings or Malcom X's. Barack had yet to take up residence in the White House. But in hip hop he found men who understood his pain. Many were fatherless and those who weren't had no father worth mentioning.

"They were telling my stories," he said. "These guys

could lead me somewhere, I thought. They could show me where I needed to be. The music was incredible. It was from my own community and spoke my own language. I found people to look up to and idolize."

Grandma wouldn't let him watch the music videos, but he still found a way. Intrigued and inspired, he decided he wanted to mimic what he saw and recreate the beauty and rhythm of hip hop.

"I started writing songs," Lecrae recalled. "My friends and I would rap them for the neighborhood kids. People started liking it. Kids at school would ask me to rap for them. I wasn't an athlete nor the scholarly student. Just a bit mischievous, a troublemaker. I wasn't the toughest guy so rap started to give me that sense of significance, that place in the world and among my peers."

The occasional hallway rap battle, constant practice and study and writing; he made rapping his world. He ate it, breathed it, slept and dreamed of it. He wanted to be everything he heard in the music.

"Ice Cube taught me how to survive in South Central. Tupac taught me what it meant to live and die in L.A., what it meant to be a gangster. I learned about weed, about drugs. I learned about everything through the music."

Lecrae's own rap took on the flavor of his music icons. Violence, girls, and money colored nearly every lyric. His heroes weren't heading to college. They weren't striving to be student-athlete of the year. They were gangsters and soon his life, not just his lyrics, started to follow in their stead. At 16, he started with weed. At 17, he quit basketball, the last remaining non-gangster holdout in his life. Drugs and partying filled the void in his search for meaning and purpose.

"I began this cycle of wanting to be somebody and wanting to be seen," he said. "It went from drinking, to drugs, to partying, to girls, to anything that might fill that emptiness, that sense of insignificance that I just couldn't shake. I was in turmoil. I didn't know my dad. I felt like my dad was this piece of my life that I needed to feel like I was somebody. The men I knew abused me, they didn't love me."

Lecrae's lyrics grew darker and his message angrier. Even when his mother moved him out of the inner city, his heart still clung to the urban life and style. Stumbling home one night, way past curfew, high and drunk, his stepfather called him out.

"Man, what are you going to do with your life?" he demanded. "You're not going to be anything at this rate. You don't care about anything."

He knew it to be true. For the first time, he saw he needed to care about something more. But what? What was the answer? He went to church with his grandmother. But the sea of grey hair, told him this wasn't for him. Church was for old people, for grandmas, not young men like himself, so he threw himself ever deeper into partying.

"As the emptiness grew more profound, I had to drink more," he admitted. "I had to smoke more. When I had to find another woman, and another woman, and another woman, I knew something must be missing, that I was headed down the wrong path."

Even his dreams were filled with torment and questions. Questions about God, needing to know if he was real, who he was, and what he wanted from him.

"I went to the library and just grabbed books about God. I was on this quest. Maybe I need God, I thought. Maybe this will give me significance. Was he Buddha? Allah? My mother wasn't even really a Christian, but she told me to read the Bible. She was just tired of my lack of direction. But I didn't want the Bible. I remember ripping out the pages and throwing them on the floor. I just couldn't wrap my hands around it being true. My pain, my sorrows, my insignificance, my burdens were just too much for me."

He wrote song after song about the emptiness and the darkness. Nothing made sense. He could find nothing to medicate the despair. He wanted anything to take away the pain, but nothing worked.

Then a friend invited him to a Bible study. He went to ask questions, to debate, and explore. It was just another step in this quest to find significance.

"It was interesting," Lecrae said, "because for the first time I saw young guys who looked like they came from where I came from. They had experienced the same things I had, knew the same idols and followed the same role models. But they loved Jesus. It seemed so weird. I thought grandmas loved Jesus. Not dudes like that."

They embraced Lecrae, accepted him, and he them, not the message or God, but the group. He latched onto the feeling of belonging. He was still a skeptic. They fed him book after book answering all the questions he could muster. After a while, he felt he belonged, that he was a "Christian" by proxy, that somehow belonging to the group and calling them friends made him whatever they were.

"But then one of them challenged me on whether I just mentally assented to the idea of God or whether I really had faith in Jesus. And that bothered me. I realized I still didn't fit in. They really loved Jesus, really believed in him. But I wasn't there yet."

Then he joined them at a Bible conference. He went more for the girls and the chance to revisit the city. But he went, nonetheless. When he arrived, he saw something totally unexpected; an arena full of people like him who just happened to love Jesus. Guys who had been shot from being in gangs, rappers, dancers, and singers all told stories of leaving their old lives to follow Jesus. People who came from the same background, lived in the same kind of neighborhoods all told this same story. They embodied the urban culture but they were all in love with Jesus. Authentically culturally urban, and authentically followers of Jesus.

"It made me wrestle," he recalled. "It made me really rethink the whole thing. It got me thinking that maybe Jesus is for real. These people were rapping about Jesus, willing to lay down their old lives, be passionate about him. If they're willing to stop wanting to be gangsters, sleep around and get drunk, there must be something to this Jesus."

Then a man stepped on stage and spoke about Jesus. He shared the message of how the Son of God became man, died on a cross, and offered forgiveness to the world. He paid a price for all sins. The price he paid was his life. Jesus died on the cross for the sins of the world, but not just for the world, for Lecrae.

"I was crushed by that. All my sin, all my lying, all my cheating, my drinking and drugging, he put it on his own back. I felt like I killed him. I felt like I did that to him. But more than that, I was bought with a price. Man, somebody thinks I'm significant enough to die for me? Somebody thinks I'm significant enough to climb up a mountain with a cross on his back, and take nails in his wrists and his feet, all that for me? And suddenly I knew. I was significant because of Jesus. It wasn't my father who never was there. It wasn't the gangster life that never filled me. It was Jesus, he alone could do it. He alone sees me as so incredibly significant that he would die for me."

His lyrics changed after that revelation. No longer did his life bleed with confusion and pain. He began to heal. He realized his significance. Jesus was a message he could share, a story he could tell. He didn't have to lose his manhood or give up his culture. Jesus had an answer. Jesus could give him significance and purpose.

> "I was created by God,
> But I don't want to be like him.
> I want to be him.
> The Jack Sparrow of my Caribbean.
> I remember the first created being,
> And how he shifted the blame on his dame
> For fruit he shouldn't have eaten.
> And I look at us all out of Eden,
> Wearing designer fig leaves
> By Luis Vuitton make believing.
> But God sees through my foolish pride.
> And that I'm weak like Adam,
> Another victim of Lucifer's lies.
> But then in steps Jesus.
> All men were created to lead,
> But we needed somebody to lead us.
> More than a teacher,
> But somebody to buy us back from the darkness.
> You could say he redeemed us."
>
> —Lecrae

It began with excitement, a thrill and a new high. He wrote up his story and began telling everyone. But the old problems and old life didn't just die off.

"I still didn't know what it meant to really follow Jesus. I didn't know that I had to lay my life down and follow him. Suddenly there were all these expectations that I couldn't live up to. I didn't know what this new life was supposed to look like. And soon the old life just crept back in. I knew it was empty, but it was all I knew. I just couldn't handle it. I went back to partying and I couldn't get out of it."

He begged God saying, "You got to get me out of this. You got to pull me out of here. I'm in a dark place. You know I'm tired of my circumstances. Do whatever you got to do to get me out of this, but just don't kill me. Don't let me die."

He soon found himself speeding down the highway, headed to the liquor store. The exit approached faster than he expected and he pulled hard to the right to make the turn. The wheels screeched, tearing under the pressure. The car skidded and then flipped, again and again. The roof collapsed. The windshield caved in. Glass and metal and plastic were everywhere. But he was safe.

"I didn't have my seat belt on, but I didn't have a scratch on me. The car was a total wreck. My glasses were bent and I had to crawl out the window to get out of the car but I was perfectly unscathed. I knew it was God. I knew at that moment that my life was in his hands.

"I decided right then to change my life. I gave him my music, started volunteering at a local juvenile detention center. I found that all the pain and hurt that I wrote into those songs spoke to these kids. All that searching for God and the need for significance, that I had written in my darkest times made them weep. They asked me to perform these songs again and again, and they wanted copies. And I realized that maybe God would use my music to speak to people, to bring change into their lives like he was bringing to mine."

Lecrae went on to release his first hip hop album, *Real Talk*, in 2004, followed two years later with *After the Music Stops*. *Rebel* launched in 2008 and landed the No. 1 spot on the Gospel chart, a first for a Christian hip hop album. September 2012 marked the release of his most successful album to date, *Gravity*, which debuted No. 3 on the Billboard 200 and won him a Grammy Award for Best Gospel Album.

Watch the Film

Lecrae
Iamsecond.com/lecrae

To see other stories like this, please visit:

Propaganda
Iamsecond.com/propaganda

Sean Little
Iamsecond.com/seanlittle

The Music Continues

An Epilogue

Brian "Head" Welch

On February 22, 2005, Brian "Head" Welch, lead guitarist for multi-platinum rock group, Korn, formally quit the band he helped form. His time with Korn brought him fame, money, and the coming true of all his wildest dreams. But with his life spiraling out of control and his daughter desperately in need of her father, Brian left the band to follow Jesus and clean up his life. Eight years later, he announced his return.

"There's a time for separation," Brian said, "and a there's a time to reconcile, and the time to reconcile is now."

It began with a chance meeting. Brian was touring with P.O.D. when they and Korn landed at the same music festival.

"I hadn't seen them in years," Brian said. "They are my brothers. I basically grew up with them since I was twelve. I figured I would just go see them. We still had good vibes for each other and it had been so long."

He soon found himself on the tour bus with Korn guitarist, James "Munky" Shaffer, who along with Brian and three others had founded Korn in 1993. Munky and Head had formed a legendary guitar duo in the early years of Korn with their dissonant and angst ridden rifts.

"We talked for 30 minutes," he said. "It was crazy emotional. By the end, he asked me to do the band meet and greet with them after the show."

He agreed. But moments before Korn got on stage, Korn bassist, Fieldy, came with another surprising invitation.

"We set up a guitar for you," he said. "Come play some songs with us."

"No way, man!" Brian said. "I'd be playing blind. I need to practice these songs."

"Well," Fieldy responded, "play blind, then."

By this point, Brian had not played with the band for seven years, a lifetime in the world of music. Fans had bemoaned the breakup of the Head-Munky guitar duo, in addition to the loss of Brian's backup vocals. Record sales for the band took a steep dive that same year as anger and confusion plagued the band's fanbase. But Brian's commitment to quit drugs, be a father to his daughter, and, above all, follow Jesus outweighed the public and private pressure to rejoin. But things had changed since then.

"There's a time to walk away and to separate yourself," Brian reflected. "But then God builds you up to be stronger than you ever been. There's a time to go back, to let the light shine."

Brian agreed to join Korn on stage for the first time since his leaving. Korn frontman, Jonathan Davis, introduced Welch to an unsuspecting crowd at the Carolina Rebellion Festival.

"For a long time, this spot right here has been very lonely—very very lonely," Davis said referring to the empty spot on stage which Brian had filled for so long. "I want to bring out one of my truest and oldest and most beloved friends to come out and have some fun with this."

The crowd roared with approval and social media soon buzzed with the news. Speculation and hope ran wild that

Brian "Head" Welch was rejoining the band. A month later, Munky called with just such an invitation.

"We are going to start writing our next record," he said. "I don't want to make this about you coming back, because I would love to see you just as my old friend, and I would love to be reconnected with you. But if you feel like you want to do this, the door's open. Let us know."

"I had a lot of concerns," Brian recalled. He had just signed onto a record label with newly rebranded band, Love and Death, and had commitments to tour with them. But above all, Brian still couldn't find room in his conscience, as a father, to play many of the band's biggest hits. Memories of his daughter skipping around the house singing, "A.D.I.D.A.S., All day I dream about sex," still rung through his head.

"Hearing her sing that song was the lowest point of my life," he said. "I knew I needed to change when I heard my little girl singing it."

The song captured the chaos that had engulfed his life at the time. His daughter proved a key motivator for his life-changing decisions. When he begged God to rescue him from his addictions and lifestyle, it was as much for himself as it was his daughter. Being a father to his daughter and a follower of Jesus remained his chief priority even with this tempting offer to rejoin the band he so loved and his brothers he so missed.

"My life was a mess, back then," he said. "But then I heard that pastor get up and say that Jesus was real, that he was so real, not just this story about a guy in a robe two thousand years ago. He's God of the universe. He said that if I invited him into my life that the bad stuff in my life would just get pushed out, that the power of God would come into my life and push everything else away. So I told God that if he was real I needed him to take the drugs away, and he did. I've never turned back since."

So even then he didn't want to be around the drugs and partying that were such a big part of the band's culture before.

"I'm all for being around people that are trying to get off drugs," he said. "But if they're happy using [drugs], I just don't like to be around that. Not that I'd fall into it, 'cause I'm done. But it's just stuff I wouldn't want me or my daughter to be around."

But despite his concerns, the scheduling and contract issues of his new band smoothed out. The band no longer even played the songs he had problems with and the drugs and partying were a thing of the past. Everyone was married. The drugs, the girls, even the alcohol were all gone.

"God speaks through circumstances," he said. "Circumstances lined up. It was like a loud voice, or a big sign that was just held up that says 'NOW!' It all seemed to fall into my lap. It was so smooth. As we talked and started playing together, it just got better, and better, and better."

"There's a time to walk away and there's a time to go back, and that's what's happening with me. I am living my destiny. I am walking in the steps ordered by the Lord for my life. I could chop my hair, and be a missionary in another country if God called me to that. No problem. I've given my life to the Lord. But he has spoken to me and led me back to my people, to hang out with them, and let the light shine."

"He's rebuilding everything in my life. The relationships with my friends are good. The reconnection with the fans are good. People are giving their lives to God. I went through a lot of difficulty during the surgery of my soul that God did over the last eight years. But when he tears down, he rebuilds. *Lord* means something like boss. So when people judge me or question my going back to the band, I just tell them to take it up with my boss."

"I'm a modern missionary, you know? I just go in there, and I play music. I hang out with my friends and love on people and God uses it all. People hear my story and God uses it to change lives. I just come and show up and the Lord uses it."

On May 15, 2013, Brian Head Welch played the first full show with Korn since his leaving eight years ago. He and the band anticipate their first new album together since 2003, later this summer.

Who Is First

God.

God is first, whether we decide to put him first or not. God makes the rules. God does not need us, but out of his love, he wants us. He depends on nothing.

People might ask, "Who made God?" The answer is no one.

Only limited things like us need a cause, a beginning. We need a mother to give us life. God doesn't need a cause.

There is no limit to God. God is beyond us, but he is also very close to us. God wants us to trust him with the heart of a child and also to love him with a mind that is maturing in wisdom.

God knows all things. God sees all things. God has all of the power.

There is only one God. But this one God is Father, Son, and Holy Spirit. Three persons all equally God, but distinct from each other. The Father is not the Son; the Son is not the Spirit. All three are distinct, but there is only one God.

God is not everything. God made everything. God is not the universe. God created the universe.

But God is also a personal being. We can have a relationship with God.

God is love. Because of his infinite love for us, he sent his

Son, Jesus, to die for us. When we trust in what Jesus did on the cross, God fills us with the Holy Spirit and we become his child.

Jesus identified with all of the miseries of mankind and took the punishment for our sins. We deserved death for our sins. But Jesus took our sins and our punishment on the cross. Jesus satisfied the wrath of God. But just as he predicted, Jesus rose from the dead on the third day.

If you trust Jesus' work on the cross for you, you will be forgiven. You will be given new life. You become a child of God.

How Do I Become Second?

Becoming second means recognizing God is first.
It is believing and trusting in Jesus and accepting who he is
and what he did. The stories in this book illustrate the peace,
purpose, and freedom that many people experienced when
they made the decision to be second. But the thread that
holds each of these stories together is not so much what they
got out of their experience but where they began.

They each began by understanding that they were broken
people. They each believed that they were sinners. Nobody
escapes the weaknesses of being human. No one is without
failures and mistakes, pride or selfishness. Everyone fails to
love as they should.

These sins or failures separate people from God. They
also bring a punishment. According to Romans 6:23, the
wages of sin is death. Because of sin everyone will face judgment when they die. "People are destined to die once and
after that to face judgment" (Hebrews 9:27). God does not

judge on whether someone did more right than wrong. Perfection is the standard. Sin at any level, any amount, makes one guilty. Even in the modern world, a person who commits a crime is not judged by whether he has done more good than he has wrong. He is judged on whether or not he committed the crime. Those who depend on their own good works are destined to spend eternity separated from God in hell.

But God offers forgiveness for all these sins. He offers forgiveness through faith in Jesus. It starts with an admission of guilt, a change of mind, a willingness to start going God's way instead of going our own way. It is admitting we are full of sin and in desperate need of help. But it is not any help we must look for, it is Jesus' help. It is Jesus we need. It is his message and sacrifice that we must accept and believe to experience forgiveness and a relationship with God. It is about faith in the God of the Bible and in his Son Jesus who came and died for the sins of the world.

So who is this Jesus?

Jesus is first. It's not about us. It's not about our good deeds or religion. It's about who Jesus is and what he did. "For what we preach is not ourselves, but Jesus Christ as Lord, and ourselves as your servants for Jesus' sake" (2 Corinthians 4:5). It's about Jesus, always and fully God, who then came to earth and was born a baby in full humanity and who later died on a cross for our sins.

Jesus died to forgive our sins. The message of Jesus is simple and is summarized in 1 Corinthians 15:1–4: "Now, brothers and sisters, I want to remind you of the gospel I preached to you, which you received and on which you have taken your stand. By this gospel you are saved, if you hold firmly to the word I preached to you . . . that Christ died for our sins according to the Scriptures, that he was buried, that he was raised on the third day according to the Scriptures." Without the death of Jesus, there would be no forgiveness of sins.

Jesus rose from the dead. The foundation of our faith is not our personal story. The foundation of our faith is a historic event: the resurrection of Jesus. Paul wrote, "And if Christ has not been raised, your faith is worthless; you are still in your sins" (1 Corinthians 15:17 HCSB).

We are saved by God's grace, not by good works. We do not earn forgiveness. It is a gift. "Now to the one who works, wages are not credited as a gift but as an obligation. However, to the one who does not work but trusts God who justifies the ungodly, their faith is credited as righteousness" (Romans 4:4–5). God expects our behavior and life to change, but this change does not save us.

We are saved by grace through faith. This gift is received through believing. "For it is by grace you have been saved, through faith—and this is not from yourselves, it is the gift of God—not by works, so that no one can boast" (Ephesians 2:8–9).

If you want to be second, if you believe in Jesus, who he is and what he did, take a moment right now and tell him. Tell him what you believe and ask him for forgiveness. Ask God to make you a part of his family.

What now?

If you have made that commitment to be second, trusted in Jesus, and accepted his forgiveness, here are some next steps for you to do.

Be baptized. Show the world you follow Jesus.

> "Baptizing them in the name of the Father and of the Son and of the Holy Spirit."
> **—Jesus, Matthew 28:19**

Love God. Love people. Live the life of second.

> "Love the Lord your God with all your heart . . . Love your neighbor as yourself."
> **—Jesus, Luke 10:27**

Commemorate Jesus. Get with other believers and remember the death of Jesus.

> "Whenever you eat this bread and drink this cup, you proclaim the Lord's death until he comes."
> **—Paul, 1 Corinthians 11:26**

Talk with God. This is a relationship. God wants to hear from you.

> "This, then, is how you should pray."
> **—Jesus, Matthew 6:9**

(For more help download our prayer guide at wearesecond. com.)

Give. Your money, time, and talents. Help the poor. Reach the lost.

> "It is more blessed to give than to receive."
> **—Jesus, Acts 20:35**

Make disciples. Teach others what God has taught you.

> "Go and make disciples . . . teaching them to obey everything I have commanded you."
> **—Jesus, Matthew 28:19–20**

I am Second is the revolutionary change in your life that starts when you put your trust in Jesus alone for your eternal life. It continues as you decide each day to put Jesus above all else. Life is a battle that is not meant to be fought alone. Discover how others like you have been set free. Be part of the revolution. Watch the films. Get involved. Join an I am Second group.

Go to www.wearesecond.com to find out how.

About the Authors

Doug Bender is an I am Second writer and small groups coach. He spends his time developing many of the small group tools found at iamsecond.com and coaching churches, organizations, and individuals to use I am Second groups to share the message of Jesus with their friends and family. He also works with I am Second's parent organization, e3 Partners, as a church planter in countries like Ethiopia and Indonesia. Doug is married to Catherine and has a one-year-old baby, Bethany.

Dave Sterrett is a speaker, missionary, and ambassador for I am Second. Dave also serves as an adjunct professor of New Testament, Philosophy, and Apologetics at Liberty University. He is the author or coauthor of several books, including, *Why Trust Jesus?*, "O" God, and the three-part novella series coauthored with Josh McDowell, The Coffeehouse Chronicles.

Acknowledgments

We would like to thank Norm Miller, whose vision and generosity started it all. A special praise goes to Adam Leydig and Nathan Sheets, whose initial creativity shaped the movement. Our deepest thanks goes to all who sat in the chair and shared their stories along with Sam Ditore and Scott Mayo whose skill in interviewing and behind the camera captured these stories along with all their fantastic crew. We thank Mike Jorgensen as ministry leader and John Humphrey as project manager for their leadership. We thank Trey Hill and Stanley Tongai for their photography.

We also appreciate e3 Partners Ministry president Curtis Hail for his guidance and wisdom all along the way and thank all the I am Second/e3 Partners staff who gave in so many ways to make this book possible. A special thanks goes to our e3 creative and events team led by Kristin Baxter and Kristin DeRight, who help make everything look great. Thanks also to our many partners, including Buddy Vaughn, Shea Pruitt, Gregg Watts, Drew Dickens, Roy Machado, Brad Dale, Kristin Cole, Joe Battaglia, Tyler Guidry, Ben Lamm, and everyone at Thomas Nelson. A special tip of the hat to our trusted literary agents Andrew and Robert Wolgemuth.

And to everyone who has interacted with I am Second,

been influenced by the films and stories, and moved to action to make the movement their own, we say thanks.

Doug Bender

To my God and Savior, Jesus, who loved me enough to call me a friend; to my wife, Catherine, and my daughter, Bethany, whose love I couldn't do without; to our team of supporters who make our ministry possible; to our editors and partners at Thomas Nelson, whose wisdom and experience made this book what it is; to my many mentors, Daniel Broyles, Dan Shelton, John Stanley, and especially Ryan Jasper and Mike Jorgensen, whose lives and wisdom have forever marked me; to my many friends and partners in ministry, especially everyone at e3 Partners and I am Second; to my family who loves me so well; to the Shelton family, whose home was always a lighthouse; to Daniel, who taught me to spend my life well; to my Texas family, the McClellans and Jorgensens; and to the man who had the courage to knock on my family's door and tell my father about Jesus, I say thanks from the bottom of my heart.

A special thanks to Albert Chu, Megan Haddox, Dylan Merlo, Nita McAdoo, Jamie Kueker, Dee Carlile, Marcia Richardson, Jeni Waldrop, Julie Ackley, and especially Amy Thase for all their help.

Dave Sterrett

I would like to thank the leadership of e3 Partners and I am Second and all of the Seconds who shared their stories. And I would like to give a special thanks to my parents, Clay and Teresa Sterrett.

"If you're at a crossroads, or if you just need some clarity
on where your life is headed and how to get there, consider
taking this book for a spin. You'll be glad you did."

–Josh Turner, double-platinum country music singer/songwriter

"This isn't just some pick-me up book, it is a way of life.
Anybody who wants to live out their full potential and purpose
should buy this book, take some time to soak in the words,
and LIVE IT!"

–Jennifer Chapman, I am Second reader

If these incredible stories of changed lives have in-spired or challenged you to reevaluate your relationship with God, then I would like to invite you to read the newest book from the I am Second movement: *Live Second: 365 Ways to Make Jesus First.*

Live Second is a daily reader with 365 readings, prayers, actions steps, and an online community of support designed as a tool for you to make truth, the Bible, and Jesus your number one priority, each and every day of the year.

The book is for anyone looking to discover meaning in life, your mission on this planet, or the cure to life's difficulties. You do not need to believe in Jesus to start this journey, but I think you will be challenged by his message before you trek too far. I believe the power of his love, the vastness of his forgiveness, and the strength of his presence will inspire you to rethink your relationship with God with each day's reading.

Each week, *Live Second* begins with an I am Second film, along with a series of discussion questions for you or your small group to think through. The remainder of the week is full of additional entries created to help you discover the meaning and application of passages from the Bible on the same topic. A brief challenge or discussion of that passage is provided, along with an action step and a Twitter hashtag enabling you to connect with others who have discussed that entry on Twitter. Many entries will also have a suggested prayer. These words will work as a guide for your conversation with God. And the last day of each week's reading will be dedicated exclusively to helping you improve your conversation time with God, ideal for those wishing to either start or reignite their relationship with God.

Wherever you find yourself today, if you are looking to take the next step with God, to explore what life can look like when he is First, then I invite you to read and experience *Live Second: 365 Ways to Make Jesus First.*

Doug Bender

Day 1: Forgive

Watch the Jeff and Cheryl Scruggs Film

iamsecond.com/
jeffandcherylscruggs

What did you like about, identify with, or learn from the Scruggses' story?

> *But we had to celebrate and be glad, because this brother of yours was dead and is alive again; he was lost and is found.*
>
> **—Luke 15:32**

Read the whole passage in Luke 15:11–32.

What It Says
1. What did you like about this passage?
2. What did you not like or find confusing about this passage?

What It Means
3. What does this passage teach about people?
4. What does this passage teach about God?

Live It. How will you live more Second today?
Tell It. How will you share what you have learned?

Practice It. Get with a friend or someone in your group. Practice or role-play your "Live and Tell" commitments.

Day 2: **Release**

Then the master called the servant in. "You wicked servant,"
he said, "I canceled all that debt of yours because you
begged me to. Shouldn't you have had mercy on your fellow
servant just as I had on you?"

—Matthew 18:32–33

Read the whole passage in Matthew 18:21–35.

    With deep wounds or unintentional annoyance, with old hurts or fresh cuts, with long struggles or slips of the tongue, whatever the case, whatever the relationship, however terrible the wrong, forgiveness is the answer. It may not be accepted. It may not change the other's behavior. It may not immediately restore the relationship. But forgiveness is what lets hurts heal, relationships begin recovery, and life to move on. Without it, loneliness will be our deepest friend, bitterness our home, and hurt our constant companion. God forgave all of our wrongs, all our sin, all our hurtful and painful offenses, all the darkness and violence, all the cruelty and neglect. He forgave it all. Surely, if God forgave every ounce of our own wrong, both secret and known, then we can forgive the comparably few wrongs that others have done to us.

Talk with God

Teach me to forgive as you have forgiven me.

Live It. How will you live more Second today?
Tell It. How will you share what you have learned?

  Tweet using #IASrelease to share your thoughts.

Day 3: Love

*"The most important commandment," answered Jesus,
"is this: 'Hear, O Israel: The Lord our God, the Lord is one.
Love the Lord your God with all your heart and with all your
soul and with all your mind and with all your strength.' The
second is this: 'Love your neighbor as yourself.' There is no
commandment greater than these."*

—Mark 12:29–31

Read the whole passage in Mark 12:28–34.

Love is not a feeling. It's not a romantic word. It's not a flip-
pant or casual word. But a God-sized word. A word that captures
all that Jesus said. All that he taught. All that he hoped to convey in
this world. It is the anthem of God. The command above all other
commands. The reason for our creation and the foundation of all
relationships. The mark of our faith and the goal of our life. It is
that thing for which we strive, that height we seek to climb, and that
purpose for which we move and breathe and live.

Talk with God

I love you. Help me love more. Mark my life with love. Fill my
breath, my steps, and my every movement with love.

Live It. How will you live more Second today?
Tell It. How will you share what you have learned?

Tweet using #IASlove to share your thoughts.

Day 4: Footwash

*Now that I, your Lord and Teacher, have washed your feet,
you also should wash one another's feet. I have set you an
example that you should do as I have done for you.*

—John 13:14–15

Read the whole passage in John 13:1–20, 34–35.

Never have feet been the pinnacle of beauty or cleanliness, but modern man has found ways to reduce much of the smell and dirtiness associated with biped locomotion. Socks and shoes, pavement and combustion engines have done wonders for the hygiene of the foot. But in the days before Nike and Reebok, before sidewalks and public transportation, feet were dirty things. The sharp smell of dust-caked feet and sun-baked funk scented the bottoms of every traveler and laborer, market shopper and street evangelist, wandering rabbi and following disciple. But despite the dirt and the smell and the humiliation, Jesus washed the feet of his disciples. The First became last. The Lord and Teacher became the servant. And he calls us to do the same. Whatever honor we have earned, whatever rights we have acquired, whatever prestige we hold, Jesus calls us to set those aside and become a servant, an example of love and humbleness. Where are the smelly feet in our world?

Talk with God

God, give me the humility to love without reward.

Live It. How will you live more Second today?
Tell It. How will you share what you have learned?

🐦 Tweet using #IASfootwash to share your thoughts.

Day 5: Love Defined

*If I speak in the tongues of men or of angels, but do not have
love, I am only a resounding gong or a clanging cymbal.*

—1 Corinthians 13:1

Read the whole passage in 1 Corinthians 13:1–8.

Love is not a line on our to-do list. It is the whole list, the
only goal, the only task in life. Love is God's defining attribute,
his all-encompassing requirement, his only law. Mastery of words,
intellect, success, power, friendship, or romance—none of these
matters without love. All of life, every good deed, every noble task,
if not colored and painted with love creates only an empty canvas.
From the mundane to the profound, from cleaning dishes to curing
cancer, nothing matters without love, and everything matters with
it. Relationships are pointless and powerless without it. Love has
little to do with feelings and everything to do with selfless, humble,
thoughtful care for another person.

Talk with God

You loved us while we were still your enemy, you died for us while
we cursed your name, and you planned our salvation knowing our
rebellion and pride. We love, because you loved first.

Live It. How will you live more Second today?
Tell It. How will you share what you have learned?

🐦 Tweet using #IASlovedefined to share your thoughts.

Day 6: Unify

*Make my joy complete by being like-minded, having the
same love, being one in spirit and of one mind.*

—Philippians 2:2

Read the whole passage in Philippians 2:1–11.

Relationships are work. Differences surface, arguments come, disagreement and fighting seem a constant threat. Being of one mind does not erase friction or conflict. It means that when differing views or desires erupt in a relationship, love wins out. Humbleness reminds us that we do not know everything and we might be wrong. Forgiveness teaches us that if Jesus forgave us for everything, then we can forgive each other for a few things. Unity calls us to remember that we are children of the same God and servants in the same kingdom. Wrapped together, practiced consistently, and held dear, these acts create love. Is love the basis of your relationships?

Talk with God

Teach me to love in such a way that makes humility, forgiveness, and unity flourish.

Live It. How will you live more Second today?
Tell It. How will you share what you have learned?

🐦 Tweet using #IASunify to share your thoughts.

Day 7: Unity

My prayer is not for them alone. I pray also for those who will believe in me through their message, that all of them may be one, Father, just as you are in me and I am in you. May they also be in us so that the world may believe that you have sent me. I have given them the glory that you gave me, that they may be one as we are one—I in them and you In me—so that they may be brought to complete unity. Then the world will know that you sent me and have loved them even as you have loved me.

—John 17:20–23

Love is the sign of our faith. Unity is the motif of our spirituality. As the Father and the Son are one, so must we be. Bitterness and resentment should have no place in our lives. Unforgiveness and prejudice should find no home in our community. Our lives and our prayers should be littered with concern for others and care for those around us.

Talk with God

Ask.

". . . that they may be one as we are one . . ."
God, I ask you to heal these relationships . . .

Tweet using #IASunity to share your prayers.

join the movement

Get involved. Join the online community, start a discussion group, get the gear, or volunteer. Find your place in the movement. Use your talents and energy to spread the stories and message of I am Second.

discover ways to get connected

connect with others

Meet us on Facebook, follow us on twitter, e-mail or live chat 24/7. Participate in praying for others or attend an I am Second event.

start a conversation

Wear the gear that is sure to start a conversation. To find everything you need to make your statement simply visit **iamsecondstore.com**.

live second every day

Get *Live Second: 365 Ways to Make Jesus First*. Read for inspiration. Do the Challenge. Change your life. **iamsecond.com/livesecondbook**

go on expedition

Go global and take the story of Jesus with you. Find out where we are headed and learn more at **iamsecond.com/expeditions**.

seconds change

I am Second films are changing lives across the world. Help bring stories and change to new audiences. **iamsecond.com/secondschange**